Praise for *The Highflier Handbook*

The book by Dr. Allen Weiner is incredibly inspiring and insightful. Allen's ability to blend anecdotes with research findings creates a compelling narrative that emphasizes the importance of strategic thinking. The numerous practical examples and stories make the concepts relatable and easy to understand. The emphasis on effective communication and the balance between strategic and tactical thinking is particularly valuable for professionals aiming to enhance their careers. Overall, Allen's work is a testament to the power of strategic thinking and its impact on the leader's personal and organizational success. This book is a must-read for anyone looking to develop their strategic mindset and improve their professional communication skills—and personal brand!

—Shola Oyewole, MBA
Vice President, Digital Innovation, UTHR

Allen Weiner is a coach's coach. I was privileged to learn from him early in my career and I'm delighted that he continues to share his wisdom so generously. He taught me that anyone can be a highflier with the right Staff Officer to teach them how—and in this book Allen does just that. His wisdom and experience are precisely what you need to elevate your career.

—Lois P. Frankel, PhD
Author of *Nice Girls Don't Get the Corner Office*

Allen Weiner is a living legend among executive coaches to the world's CEOs. *The Highflier Handbook* translates his wisdom into concrete tips and examples you can put into practice immediately. The book is packed with time-tested research on communication and leadership. More importantly, the tips Weiner offers have been road-tested with thousands of highflier clients over the decades and are illustrated in the book with the help of interviews with top industry leaders. Weiner teaches you much more than improving mere appearances or adding polish through superficial behaviors.

Weiner shows you how to think more strategically, speak with authentic substance, and make your point with credibility. In short, this book will help you establish a genuine leadership presence and become the highflier you were meant to be.

—Alex Lyon
Professor, Author, Executive Coach, and YouTube Creator

I cannot think of anyone better to write a book on highfliers than the ultimate highflier himself, Allen Weiner. And quite literally: from his days in the U.S. Navy serving on destroyers and cruisers, Allen has worked alongside some of the world's highest fliers, and his real-world experience makes him peerless in the world of executive coaching. As a leader, there is no more vital differentiator between good and great than the ability to communicate effectively. It's why Allen's first book, *So Smart But ...*, has become mandatory reading for any new hire in my organization. In that book, Allen gifts us with the strategies and tools required to ace any engagement, and *The Highflier Handbook* will take readers from the skies to the stratosphere.

—Ali Mohamadi
Vice President, Medical Affairs North America, Vertex Pharmaceuticals

I've worked with Allen for more than 25 years in helping me develop strong executives into truly great ones. He knows leadership communications like no one else. In this book, he really brings to life what distinguishes the best of the best. Buy this book, read it, then read it again and again.

—Curt Roberts
President, SonderMind

THE
HIGHFLIER
HANDBOOK

THE
HIGHFLIER
HANDBOOK

HOW TO BE SEEN
AND BECOME
A LEADER
AT WORK

ALLEN N. **WEINER**

Foreword by **DON ROBERT**
Chairman, London Stock Exchange Group

WILEY

Published by John Wiley & Sons, Inc., Hoboken, New Jersey.
Published simultaneously in Canada.

For general information on our other products and services or for technical support, please contact our Customer Care Department within the United States at (800) 762-2974, outside the United States at (317) 572-3993 or fax (317) 572-4002.

Wiley also publishes its books in a variety of electronic formats. Some content that appears in print may not be available in electronic formats. For more information about Wiley products, visit our website at www.wiley.com.

Library of Congress Cataloging-in-Publication Data is Available:

ISBN: 9781394306046 (Hardback)
ISBN: 9781394306060 (ePDF)
ISBN: 9781394306053 (ePub)

Cover Design: Wiley
Cover Image: © Worawut Prasuwan/Getty Images
Author Photo: © Curt Sletten

SKY10098761_022125

Family First

To Carol

To Matt and Sarah

The only direction Hitchcock gave the actress Eva Marie Saint was to "do three things: lower your voice; don't use your hands; and look into Cary's eyes at all times." If Saint had considered the techniques she learned at the Actor's Studio sacrosanct, she might have mocked such simple suggestions. The techniques worked magically, in part because they were far more revealing of character than they might appear.

—Hitchcock's Blondes by Laurence Leamer

Contents

Foreword

O ver the course of my career as a manager, CEO, chairman, board member, executive coach, and technology investor I've seen dozens of promising colleagues come and go. Nearly all of them have enviable qualities that are evident right from the start. Impressive intellect, big capacity for work, and polished communication skills are a few that come to mind. In a world of fast-paced, competitive, tech-enabled business, these qualities are now regarded as the price of admission.

Occasionally someone will stand out from the crowd, clearly exhibiting these qualities and many more, making me want to nurture them, promote them, back them, and catch their energy. These are the highfliers, and they are the subject of this groundbreaking book.

So, what's the difference between a talented professional and a highflier? A comparative discussion about two interns with Harry, my first tough-love manager, has stayed with me to this day. Ron was bright, personable, hardworking, and very capable. Darryl showed the same qualities, but was also polished, forward-thinking, and able to solve complex operational problems. In summing up the difference between the two Harry said to me, "Ron might get there first, but Darryl will go a lot farther." Without using the label, he was describing the essence of a highflier. Who's the flash in the pan, and who's the future CEO? Understanding what a highflier looks like is the first step in the journey to becoming one.

Foreword

Allen Weiner is the maestro of understanding and teaching the essential components of winning leadership behaviors. His life work has focused on the scientific and practical applications of communications effectiveness as the flywheel of career success. Allen's seminal work, *So Smart But...*, now stands alone in the crowded field of leadership teaching. His insights and "tips & tricks" have helped thousands of talented people find shortcuts to achieving their true potential. I'm one of the grateful beneficiaries of Allen's wisdom.

Allen Weiner has had a significant impact on my own career success and on many of the people I've worked with along the way. Many years ago, he was parachuted in to help improve my communication skills. Left untreated, this issue could have derailed my early career success. I was teetering on the edge of being a highflier and I credit Allen with pushing me over the top. Since then, I have brought Allen in to most of the companies I've been involved with to work with promising colleagues in need of that final push.

Allen has now turned his attention to this previously unexplored area of career potential ... the highflier. This book answers the big questions: How do you spot a highflier? How does a highflier behave? Why are highflier behaviors important? And how does the highflier attract the attention of their CEO? In my experience, the rewards that come to the highflier more than justify the small investment in buying and studying this book: better career prospects, more rapid promotions, early C Suite exposure, and financial rewards.

The Highflier Handbook should become a bedside reference to anyone seeking to get an edge and accelerate their career success. I have already started to incorporate its insights in my executive coaching practice.

Congratulations on taking this important step in going farther and faster!

Don Robert
—Chairman of London Stock Exchange Group

Preface (and a Personal Note to the Reader)

I suspect you're reading *The Highflier Handbook* because either you are a highflier or aspire to be a highflier.

One of the first messages I heard from Dr. James McCroskey and Dr. Michael Burgoon when I started the Communication Studies program at West Virginia University stayed with me. "Your client is one person. The individual is the unit of analysis," they said. "You may be asked to do a program on 'Team Communication' or 'Organizational Communication.' But you'll be evaluating individuals when the process begins."

There are resources for an entire organization like McKinsey and Company or Bain or Boston Consulting Group. And they are wonderful at what they do. I have met many, many of them and am blown away by what they bring to their clients. But *you* are my one and only concern. If you are at the top of your game, others will have benefitted from being around you and that will make them better. In other words, I start from the inside out, so to speak, believing that one person, a leader, can spread his or her abilities around the organization and inspire greatness. So, if you are encouraged to "work with a coach" or to attend a program on leadership, jump with your whole heart on the opportunity you have been offered.

Not long ago, a seminar participant said, "I don't understand why this organization puts so much effort into programs on what I call 'charm school.'"

I smiled and said, "You know, even if that were the impetus behind bringing me here, which I assure you it is not, a day spent helping you to be charming isn't exactly an obsession with what is often called soft skills. The prefix *char* in *charming* appears in *character*. It also appears in *charisma*. You'll get a lot out of this day if you think of it that way."

Each chapter in this book stands on its own as a resource for you. I could not be more flattered than I am knowing I might be a resource for you. You are the "individual who is my unit of analysis."

Introduction

I couldn't make up my mind which of two stories I should start *The Highflier Handbook* with, so I'm going to tell you both.

First, one Friday in December, I had led a communication seminar in Long Beach, California. As I was packing up, the CEO passed the conference room on his way out. He walked in and sat down, and we exchanged holiday wishes. He then said, "There's something I want to make sure you tell everyone who attends these programs. So often people come into my office for a meeting. They start talking about ideas. Their style of speaking reminds me of a drum solo at a jazz club. They are fast and often all over the place. I want them to practice speaking in an organized way so I can follow the train of thought."

Isn't that a terrific analogy? The *rat-a-tat-tat* of a drum solo. That's just one example of a behavior that can undermine an otherwise brilliant employee in the mind of a senior member of the leadership team. Here in *The Highflier Handbook*, you'll read about ways to avoid this and other unintentional behaviors to make certain you are seen as you would want to be seen.

Next: In my last year at USC and just before graduation, one of my professors asked me if I'd like to accompany him to a speech he was asked to give. One of the fraternities asked him to speak about communication and leadership. I was to act as his gofer. Merriam-Webster says a gofer is an employee whose duties include running errands. And I was happy to do it. At that point I had not actually decided to be a consultant. The general path for a PhD graduate like me in Communication Studies was to apply for a professorship at a different academic program. But something changed my mind.

The president of the fraternity introduced my "boss" and said, "Today we'll get some suggestions on how we can show leadership to the Interfraternity Council." He continued by saying, "For instance, how can I show more leadership among the brothers when there are major disagreements?"

The first thing I heard the professor say was, "I'm not here to give you tips about leadership. What I'm going to do is lay out some communication theory and ideas." In other words, he was going to conduct what would amount to the class he taught.

I thought to myself, "Here's someone who wants some suggestions on how to do something better and the professor either won't do it or can't do it." That afternoon, I decided to do what I've spent my career doing: advising clients on how to become more effective communicators with maximum credibility who are destined for leadership roles.

The Highflier Handbook will lay out for you just what those techniques and strategies are. You'll read examples here from C Suite executives that will raise your level of awareness of what works well and what doesn't. I've devoted my practice to the job of helping clients impress their colleagues with their speaking and written abilities. It's this impulse to help that led to my first book, *So Smart But... : How Intelligent People Lose Credibility—and How They Can Get it Back* (Jossey-Bass 2006), and now this one.

If you consistently apply the strategies I give you in this book, someone soon will point you out and say, "That's a highflier."

Chapter 1

Incredibly Talented

I knew from the beginning that I was looking at a highflier.

Why Me? Why Allen Weiner?

Of course, I always introduce myself at the start of a seminar, so it seems proper to start *The Highflier Handbook* the same way. The question has always been, "How did you become an opinion leader on executive communication? What gives you the bona fides to be an advice giver about these issues?"

For any of you who knew you had a knack for something early, maybe it was musical talent or writing or auto mechanics, I started picking up on communication behavior while working for my dad in retail. I was 12 years old when I first began helping him at his store. I picked up on facial expression and body language and ways that people expressed themselves. I was fascinated by all of that. I didn't know at that time how I would turn what I saw into a profession. I just knew I was pretty good at it. You could call what I was seeing as learning sales skills if listening and watching customers is at the heart of sales. And most sales professionals would agree.

My first chance to study communication in an academic setting was as a Communication major in college. I was lucky in that it was an immersion in rhetoric and public address. What I had picked up on my own was validated by studying the classic rhetoricians like Aristotle and the application of those principles in presidential rhetoric as Abraham Lincoln used it and finally as all speech writers today apply them.

When I finished school, I joined the Navy. I served on a destroyer and then a cruiser. I was assigned to the Officer of the Deck when out at sea and reported courses and speeds and weather conditions. I was given a lot of advice about how to properly perform my duties. That was an early lesson in simplicity and clarity. But more than proper communication, it was the experience that led me to realize how I flourished in a support role. Even now, when a new client tells me how happy they are to have an executive coach, I tell them, "I'd rather you think of me as your staff officer for communication, credibility, and leadership issues. Think of me as reporting to you and ready to offer advice and counsel when you need it."

I returned to school for a Master's Degree in Communication Studies, as it was then called. The thesis requirement was a disciplined research study. Mine was on Machiavellianism or a personality quality that loves to influence others for the sheer joy of the exercise. I learned statistics and how to conduct proper scholarly research.

I then went to the University of Southern California for a PhD in Communication and was a large part of the Center for Communication Research and Service. Another two years of thorough and disciplined study.

I opened my own firm, Communication Development Associates (CDA), Inc., the day after graduation. I've been all over the world offering advice and counsel to clients who knew how important credible communication behavior would be in their careers.

That, in short, is the road I've been on that led to this book, *The Highflier Handbook*.

Why Now? Why Should You Care?

I have built a career determined to help fliers become highfliers. I simply had a calling, it's fair to say. I wanted to look back someday and be proud of the role I might have played in others' careers. CDA's practice has, from the start, based our efforts on senior-level feedback about aspiring leaders. Early on employees would receive mid-year and end-of-year reviews that included insights about their performance ranging from "needs to improve," to "met expectations" to "exceeds expectations." In addition, a phenomenon is now a regular exercise throughout corporate America called "360's." I'll wager that most of you reading this have participated in a 360 exercise. Impressions about people were sought from those who report to the person requesting them, from their peers, and from those to whom they reported. The impressions were often about demonstrated competence. For instance, "An incredible contributor," "A proven scientific mind," or "Shares both tactical and strategic ideas to all levels." And, of course, in the sections labeled "Needs Improvement," one might read, "Needs to speak up more in meetings," or "Doesn't participate in team activities," and the dreaded "Not a team player."

At some point, an employee might be encouraged to work with an executive coach to gain some ideas and suggestions to improve their performance. I was among those often chosen to be that coach.

Since the vast majority of the feedback began with very high praise for someone's intellect or demonstrated brain power followed by not so high praise for their communication behavior, I decided to catalog many of those impressions in my first book, *So Smart But ....: How Intelligent People Lose Credibility—and How They Can Get it Back*.

I was always interested, however, in how some employees made excellent first impressions. It may have been in an interview. It could have been skills shown at a presentation. It very well may have been in a team meeting where ideas were flying around. I knew I was privileged to hear about these stories from some of the world's most discerning and successful executives. I realized I had to share their thoughts, their observations, with as many people as possible. And that has led to *The Highflier Handbook: How to Be Seen and Become a Leader at Work.*

The interviews you will read in each of these chapters were carefully chosen. "Curated" is a popular descriptor now and I think it applies to how I chose the people I interviewed. They are all Hall of Famers, you might say. I knew I was the keeper of a treasury of ideas offered about highfliers. If any of us were to take a class at which all of my interviewees were speakers, it would be the experience of a lifetime—to say nothing of the fee all of them would so richly deserve. These executives have shown the ability to identify highfliers within their organizations and had experienced being seen as highfliers themselves. They know what it takes. *The Highflier Handbook* is my way of helping you to become a highflier, too. To that end, along with the interviews you will see the tips and tools (TNTs) I have given to clients to help them all get to the next step along their career path.

"I knew from the start that I was looking at a highflier."

In *The Future Leader*, Jacob Morgan describes asking CEOs, "How do you define leadership?" He relates their total ambiguity about it. He says, "The most common response was 'Hmmm, nobody's ever asked me that before.'" He adds:

> *"We just take the concept of a leader for granted and assume that we all know what that looks like and who is a great leader. It's a bit like trying to define water; it sounds silly because, after all, we all know what water is, right? But how would you define water to someone who has never seen it? Would you just say it's a clear tasteless liquid? Dozens of liquids are clear and tasteless. Leadership is the same;*

6

it's everywhere in some form and we experience it daily, whether at work, playing sports, watching TV or shopping. It's all around us like air, and as a result we never stop to question what it really is or who a leader is. That's how exasperating books on leadership have come to be. We can't get specifics on how to be one."

—*(Morgan 2020)*

So many of my conversations with established leaders began when I took a call from one or another about someone they had encouraged to work with me. But these conversations always included a "but." From what I learned working with senior leaders in my earlier years, the "but" they usually talked about always involved (and still does) communication behavior. I wrote all about this in my first book, *So Smart But ….: How Intelligent People Lose Credibility—and How They Can Get It Back* (2006).

I've heard all about what they think leadership looks and sounds like, and it didn't come from interviews. We were very often sitting around and talking about people who worked in their organization. All their stories about impressive people had something to do with communication behavior. It was statements like, "She took the bull by the horns in that meeting and had a no-nonsense quality to her words." Here, in *The Highflier Handbook*, I'm going to share many more of those discussions in order to make the point that, overwhelmingly, people know a leader when they see or hear one.

Logos, Pathos, Ethos

We all owe our original understanding of what makes people credible, and what doesn't, to Aristotle. Aristotle described the qualities speakers needed to sway the crowd. I learned those qualities as an undergraduate major in Rhetoric and Public Address at West Virginia

University (WVU). However, one would be hard pressed to find a discussion of those rhetorical qualities at a college major these days. All the academic programs now are identified as "Communication Studies." In fact, my PhD from the University of Southern California reads exactly that: Communication Studies. It was just a lucky confluence of timing that I have been able to study in both programs.

Rhetoric is fascinating to me. Have you ever wondered why Abraham Lincoln, in the Gettysburg Address, said, "Government of the people, by the people, for the people, shall not perish from the earth"? Did you ever wonder why he just didn't say, "Government of and by and for the people"? Probably not. Well, it's because he read classical rhetoric and knew the power of repeating the same word at the end of three phrases.

But first, Aristotle. He described three qualities that a speaker needs to be successful with an audience: Logos, ethos, and pathos.

- *Logos* appeals to the audience's reason. It's the study of creating logical arguments.

- *Ethos* appeals to a person's status when you hear him or her speak and how that helps build a sense of trust.

- *Pathos* is about emotions and how a speaker attempts to make listeners feel anger or even love.

To show you how much immeasurable impact Aristotle still has, speaker, advisor, and author Chunka Mui used the acronym SWAN to describe Gordon Bell in a lovely obituary. I'll leave it to you to learn more about Gordon, who was an engineer. Here is what Chunka wrote in a post on LinkedIn:

"Gordon embodied what we aimed for in all our recruiting; Gordon was a SWAN: he was smart, worked

---

hard, and nice. He also brought his considerable gravitas and sound advice to the Exchange, a sort of 'Vanguard 2.0,' a senior executive learning program where Diamond brought together technology and business executives to explore and exploit the strategic opportunities enabled by rapidly accelerating digital technologies. And Gordon was always a willing early reader of my book and article drafts. Adept as ever at zeroing in on the weakest points of my arguments, his comments always made my work better."

Here's how Aristotle's model generally applies to SWAN:

- Logos (Smart): Chunka wrote, "Adept at zeroing in on weak points of my arguments." Aristotle said, "Appeals to the audience's reason."
- Ethos (Worked hard): Chunka wrote, "He … worked hard. … Gordon was always a willing early reader of my book and article drafts." Aristotle said, "Appeals to the speaker's status or authority, making the audience more likely to trust them."
- Pathos (and Nice): Chunka said Gordon was "nice." Aristotle said, "A speaker appeals to the emotions."

From Ethos to Credibility

Now, on to the beginning of social science research on credibility and the beating heart of *The Highflier Handbook*. After leaving the U.S. Navy in 1970, I returned to Morgantown, West Virginia, to begin a master's degree in Speech.

I need to quickly say about my time serving that a large part of it included reporting to the captain of my ship on the bridge, the USS Newport News. Even though this book focuses entirely on leadership, I became addicted to serving the captain and to this day think that experience led me to being an advisor now. Many times, I've told prospective clients who ask me to describe what we will be doing together that I am not fond of the term "executive coach." It implies that I'm senior to my client. Just as I was junior to the captain, I like thinking of myself as junior to my client and acting as his or her advisor. So, I've always said, "Think of me as your staff officer for credibility issues. I report to you and serve at your pleasure."

Now, during the time I was in the service, the entire Speech Department and most of the professors in it, the Rhetoric and Public Address part, was, you might say, "relieved of duty" and replaced by professors who had studied under David K. Berlo at Michigan State University and were his acolytes. I was a convert on the first day after my first class. The Communication Studies Department was born.

Instead of memorizing Aristotle's Rhetoric (I'd done that already), I became involved in a disciplined study of this magic term "credibility." Social science means statistics. Statistics means math and things like multiple regression analysis. It's rare for liberal arts students to gravitate to math. However, I could not get enough of it. Just the idea that I could be a part of a scientific analysis of what makes us all come across credibly, and that I could confidently expose potential clients to that, made it so exciting.

Why tell you that? It's to give you added confidence that the advice you get in this book has a foundation of pure no-nonsense research. Years of it. This is not YouTube and TikTok and LinkedIn purveyors of random beliefs about eye contact and hand gestures.

I remember another esteemed professor of mine, Mike Burgoon, taking a deep draw of a cigarette one evening and saying, "You are not in a trade school. This is an Arts and Sciences program. You have a responsibility to others to make claims based on science." My enthusiasm for the study of communication began here.

Early Research and Testing on Credibility

David K. Berlo was the first name I heard as I started my master's and where my studies of communication began. He published a piece in *The Public Opinion Quarterly* (1969) entitled "Dimensions for Evaluating the Acceptability of Message Sources." To paraphrase Berlo's words: It partly depends on who said it. We can call it ethos, charisma, or "source credibility." But the more of "it" the communicator is perceived to have, the more likely it will be taken seriously. Typically, "credibility" depends on issues like social status. So it's not subject to change.

This was Aristotle on steroids. The words themselves were blowing apart the traditional beliefs about the impact of a person's behavior on his or her credibility and ability to be an effective contributor. But most importantly … it had been tested! And, by the way, "tested" means posing hypotheses, having subjects involved in a simulation, asking them to complete questionnaires about their experience, submitting those to computer tests, and waiting breathlessly for the results.

Berlo was on the faculty at Michigan State University and went on to become the President of Illinois State University. He was among the first to be described as an American communication theorist. That's what I wanted to be called!

Five Factors of Leadership

I was fortunate enough to begin my study and research in communication at exactly the year that two of Berlo's students came to join the faculty of the new Communication Studies Department at West Virginia. One was chosen to be the chair of the program, Jim McCroskey, and the other was a full professor, Mike Burgoon (the cigarette smoker).

I remember asking Dr. Burgoon one evening after reading B.F. Skinner's book *About Behaviorism* when I could think of myself as a behaviorist.

He said, "When you believe it." I believed it.

According to Tim Levine and Hee Sun Park, McCroskey had a prolific research career (Levine and Park 2017). His research made many substantial contributions to the field of communication. In the most recent analysis of in-field journal articles, Jim was credited with 170 articles compared to the second-ranked prolific author. Jim's website lists 55 books and 240 research articles. Now, this is telling: What is less well known these days is that Jim's publications began with articles with titles such as "The Effect of College Speech Training on Academic Marks."

McCroskey had his mind on the impact of communication on success even 60 years ago. I was just so lucky timing wise to be introduced to credibility and success at the very beginning of my journey into consulting. Levine and Park note that McCroskey was one of the editors of *Human Communication Research* (HCR). My first published study appeared in Volume 1, Number 1: "The Effect of Interaction Behavior on Source Credibility, Homophily, and Interpersonal Attraction" (McCroskey, Hamilton, and Weiner 1974).

And that brings us to this: Ultimately those studies revealed five qualities or factors that were at the heart of a person's ability to influence others. That phrase, "a person's ability to influence others" is a fine, if partial, definition of LEADERSHIP.

Those five factors are: Competence, Composure, Character, Sociability, and Extroversion. A sixth factor was subsequently found that McCroskey called Goodwill. In other words, all the feelings and attitudes and perceptions you have of the people you interact with most likely are related to these as well as their perceptions of you. And we have so much quantitative evidence for that.

A statistical test called Factor Analysis is generally used to take all the various adjectives people use to describe us and group them into categories. You may very well use different words, but all the words fall somewhere in these categories.

- When you say, "Jack is so smart," you are in the competence bucket, so to speak. If you think "Jack is in over his head," it's in that bucket but unfortunately in the wrong direction.

- The most common request I have received over the last few years to do coaching or seminars at the corporate level involved "executive presence." That is the modern term for composure.

- If you think you can trust Jane for reasons you can't quite describe but you know it when you see it … that's character.

- After you interview someone for a position and talk to others about your impressions, it's very possible you'll say, "I really liked him. I want you to meet him." If so, that's what McCroskey called sociability and I've always called likeability.

- Finally, have you ever started to fall asleep in a meeting because some of the participants rarely spoke or when they did speak were so low in volume you had to slap yourself to stay awake? The opposite of that is extroversion, which I have renamed high energy. I'll talk more about the textbook definition of extroversion as we move forward in this book. But trust me at this point, the primary outward behavior as observed by others is energy. If you have a lot of energy, someone is going to call you extroverted. That has been my experience during my career in consulting. "Extroverted" is loosely used to describe things like, "She grabbed the mike and took over that meeting."

Myers and Briggs may tell you, "You don't know what you're talking about. That has nothing to do with our program," but you'll think to yourself, "If it walks like a duck..."

There will be interviews to come in *The Highflier Handbook* that will give us plenty of additional information about these factors, including the Goodwill factor.

Competence, Trustworthiness, and Caring

When I completed the master's thesis and program at WVU, I left for the Doctoral program at the University of Southern California. My first class there was with another exceptional scholar (and gentleman), Dr. Ken Sereno, who has now retired. His research confirms and piggybacks on McCroskey's findings. Regarding the factors just laid out, Ken contributed these thoughts in an interview with me:

> *"Speakers do not HAVE credibility. Credibility is a perception that listeners attribute to a speaker. Many politicians, for instance, will be viewed as highly credible to some. They would not be held in such high esteem by others. Character is a measure of trustworthiness. There are two aspects. First, the speaker is believable. We trust him or her to tell the truth. Second, the speaker is reliable and dependable. When they say they are going to do something, you can count on it. Regarding 'Goodwill,' I like to call it Caring. Why do I say that? Well, it's important. 'No one cares what you know until they know you care.'"*

The factors differ in ranking depending on the situation. Competence may not always be the most important. Caring is more important when comforting a friend. How do speakers create, maintain, and raise perceptions of their competence, trustworthiness, and caring? That last question will be answered by several executives here in *The Highflier Handbook*. So let's take them one at a time starting with competence. (I go into even more detail on competence in Chapter 3.)

Breadth, Depth, Height, and Sight

Recently, one of my clients, a CEO with an organization involved in a nationwide platform that puts nurses at the bedside of every patient in need, wrote that one of the employees who jumped out to him as impressive "...sought to produce outcomes rather than output in every aspect of their early work." Another "made courageous public statements about needed process changes to ship the app better in their first company-wide town hall."

I want you to notice that these two compliments are about intellect, and not about style. They are comments that put thinking and acting first. That's competence. In my first book, I wrote that no one has smarter clients than I do. As committed as I am to great advice about style as well, no one is more admiring of intellectual firepower than I am.

Google the term *competence*. "The ability to do something successfully or efficiently." In addition, "A speaker's subconscious intuitive knowledge of the rules of their language." Or look up *intellect*: "The ability to acquire and apply knowledge and skills." Or "...the collection of information of military or political value." Let's just call it "the collection of information of value."

I told a group recently when talking about "what is value?" that there are three types of information your C level executives and board members will think of as "information of value." Those three revolve around these imperatives: faster, cheaper, and better. Here's a sample of an actual message I want you to use at work. Consider it my first gift to you:

"We'll be early to market. We'll produce more revenue than we projected in our most recent plan, and finally, we'll create real value for our customers and stockholders."

Another "T and T" (Tip and Tool, or TNT; they're explosive!) I want to offer you early here in the book is this: Over the course of your career, and there's no time like early in your career, you have a chance to show four aspects of your competence in every meeting. Those four I've labeled *breadth, depth, height,* and *sight.*

- Breadth reflects the various issues associated with a topic. You may say, "There are three issues to consider." But if you say, "We need to think about cost, delivery, and reliability," you bring a breadth of your analysis and thinking to the conversation.

- If, on the other hand, in a different meeting you say, "I'll give you an example of what I mean when I say 'delivery,'" you are adding depth to the topic. All statistics and examples show your depth of knowledge on that topic.

- In another meeting, you could have a chance to raise the level of thinking to a higher plane—a more strategic plan. You might say, "We're here to solve a cost problem. But let's not take our eyes off the prize, which is our ability to sustain our competitive advantage. That's what this is all about." That's you reaching higher. And I call that "height."

- Finally, in yet another meeting, especially at the conclusion, you could say, "If all goes well, I see this getting us to our goal by this time next year." Here you are projecting your "sight," or willingness to look ahead. That's yet another sign of strategic thinking. It's also at the heart of the compliment that you have "vision."

Breadth, depth, height, and sight. It's a surefire way of demonstrating how much competence you have and are willing to share in a team meeting.

Keep in mind that you don't have to make a speech about it. You're simply talking about it in a meeting. In addition, I encourage you to "piggyback" on what someone else says with the same notion in mind. If one team member says, "Those are the issues as I see them," you should say, "To piggyback on what Ashley just said, I think another issue is _____." That is you adding breadth to the conversation. If Jason says, "It's mostly a matter of customer satisfaction," you should piggyback on that by saying, "I talked to Matt Smith about that just yesterday. He said, 'We just completed a survey and 80% of our suppliers are thrilled with it,'" then you are adding depth. Depth leads to compliments like, "You really know about this at a very detailed level."

I want you all to watch the reactions that people have to your messages in a meeting. If you can see your listeners live or on Zoom, test this: After you offer up that statistic, your listeners will nod their head. If you can't see them, you'll most likely hear them say, "Really," or "Good work," or "Didn't know that." That's the power of factual statements like statistics. So often my clients have worried about how little reaction they were getting from others at a meeting. I've often said, "They aren't going to react out of the kindness of their heart. You have to make them react. Factual statements create reactions."

This is a good place to put all this in perspective as it relates to the ultimate prize: How to be seen and become a leader at work. When you offer statements, oral or written, that show the breadth and depth of your thinking, you'll be immediately seen as competent. Competence, as we've seen, is one of the, if not the, most important factors in perceptions of credibility. Credibility is a required factor for you to be described as a potential leader early in your career.

Here's what Jeff Weiss told me. Jeff is a Co-founder and Managing Director of the Center for Corporate Innovation in Los Angeles. In a description of one person that Jeff's organization invited to speak that illustrates what I've said to you earlier, Jeff said:

> *"Some people pick up these leadership skills, try it and develop them on their own. In talking about healthcare and the need for clear differentiation of value, this speaker put it in the context of his company, which was this big healthcare system all over the Midwest. He said, 'All the different cultures need to act as one. They need to integrate and agree to one system. They all must do it. They need to speak the same way.'"*

Can you see the breadth of his thinking here? He started at a high level, brought it down to his company, and then "brought it down to the task." This is an example of coming across as strategic. And there will be much more about strategic thinking and perceptions of leadership in this book. This is also an example of problem-solving steps. More on this to come as well.

In the introduction, I described a CEO who told me people often talk in a way that reminds him of a drum solo. Jeff described the same guest speaker he hosted, as discussed earlier, as outlining his message and gave me this example: "There are three points I'm going to focus on today. Those ideas are current research, how that fits within different cultures, and finally success stories. I'll take them one at a time." This "outlining" makes it so much easier for the listener to follow the speaker's train of thought. It differentiates the speaker from anyone else who doesn't speak this way. If this speaker is lucky, it's not a stretch to suggest that not only does it make him sound clearer, it also makes him sound competent. That is a small price to pay to generate such a grand perception.

Competence Is at the Head of the List

I decided to make the last interview in this chapter one that placed nearly 100 percent of this CEO's prize quality on competence. Bill Sibold served as Executive Vice President, Specialty Care of Sanofi and President, Sanofi North America. Sanofi's 10,000 employees focus on five specialty therapeutic areas including Immunology, Oncology, Rare Disease, Rare Blood Disorders, and Neurology. Previously, Bill served as Chief Commercial Officer of Avanir Pharmaceuticals, President and CEO of Lycera Corp, Senior Vice President of U.S. Commercial for Biogen, and is currently Chief Executive Officer of Madrigal Pharmaceuticals.

Here is what Bill told me:

"People like the one I am going to tell you about become experts. It is not essential that the expertise be on something big and complicated. It may be a smaller part of something big. They are looked at as the expert and they grow from that. As to communication skill, their knowledge in both depth and breadth on a topic allows them to show their approach and judgment. All of us have to transfer our knowledge to others very efficiently. Frankly, that's how they are going to be judged. But if they don't have the underlying competence, you can very quickly find out the someone is just not so good.

The person I so well remember, from the first meeting, was simply so well prepared ... so well prepared! They knew all about the topic that we were talking about at the meeting. They were deep in it and understood it. They could express what was important and not important. The thing that made me even more interested in this person was they were someone who I respected and endorsed. I told various people, 'This is someone you should look at.' A third party endorsement like that helps to accelerate their value rather than trying to scratch the value out.

Right off the bat anyone could tell they were smart, well trained, prepared, and knew the detail. And the big plus: you could communicate clearly with them. They were a project of mine for 12 years. They are gone and have done their own thing now. I was crushed when they left. They were so remarkable. I could always trust that if they were doing something, if I asked them to do something, it would be done thoroughly.

I would like to add something about the way this person, and all of the people you call highfliers, handle clarifying questions. They are typically specific to the topic. They show an understanding of the topic by the ability to answer in a full way in addition to the requested fact. You get a context too. I get an answer and when I ask the next question, they are ready to answer that one as well.

Here's an example. If I asked what's the distribution look like across the country, I get a number and that is incredibly reassuring. The big thing here is trust. I trust what they've said and what they are going to say. There is nothing like demonstrating that one has answers to questions I have asked.

I also appreciated their ability to go from zero feet to 30,000 feet. The pace with which they were able to change altitudes was impressive. Some people say, 'Well, I'll come back and talk about that later.' But those who can float up and down, go to detail or step back and put it in the context of the whole picture, are very, very hard to find. This one was so professional in the ability to be professional and not offensive. The style was one that was simply accepted. There are not a lot of people like that, right?"

Chapter 2

Executive Presence

He exuded a level of composure unusual in someone so recently out of an MBA program.

A s I was preparing my notes for this book, I reviewed our archives to identify and analyze the most cited reason(s) given to engage our firm for executive coaching and/or executive seminars. Overwhelmingly, "learning more about executive presence or gravitas" took the number one spot. Here's an example of a program description our seminar host sent participants to prepare them for the experience:

> *"You will be participating in a two-day seminar that has executive presence as its main focus. You will learn about executive presence and how it fits into the broader model of credibility and leadership."*

In another example, the HR VP who reached out to us about a one-to-one engagement for an employee said: "We think of gravitas as a cornerstone of a leader. The person we're recommending to work with you doesn't come across as a leader who inspires his team and we learned about it in a recent survey. He spoke at a recent town hall. He'd been with us for a month. He needs to inspire trust early with a commanding presence."

A piece about executive presence in 2023 from Management Consulted stated that everyone knows "people who have an undeniable 'pizzazz,' an attractive flair or charisma to them that is appealing. They walk into the room and know how to command attention, as well as how to empower others. They instill confidence in teams and clients' confidence in their own abilities and the broader vision. These people have what we like to call executive presence. The good news is that it is a learned skill—meaning anyone can develop it!" In this chapter, you find out how.

Being a Presence in the Room

Let's begin with some science and studies. Sylvia Ann Hewlett of Thrive Street Advisors in Washington, DC, reported on a study of executive presence, or EP. She wrote, "We learned that EP rests on three pillars: How you act (gravitas), How you speak (communication), and How you look (appearance)." (Hewlett 2024)

The report went on to say, "Some 67 percent of the 268 senior executives we surveyed said that gravitas is what really matters. Signaling that 'you know your stuff cold,' that you can go 'six questions deep' in your domains of knowledge, is more salient than either communication (which got 28 percent of the senior executive vote) or appearance (which got a mere 5 percent)."

In a section Thrive Street Advisors called "Showing Teeth," they noted, "CTI research finds that 70 percent of leaders consider decisiveness to be a component of EP for both men and women, second only to confidence in a crisis, making it a core aspect of gravitas. Being able to make decisions isn't so much the issue as needing to appear decisive in public—the difference, again, between doing the job of a leader and *looking* like one as you're doing it, between demonstrating competence and exuding *presence*."

The recognition of the importance of executive presence in leadership development has been growing over the years. A study by the Center for Talent Innovation (now called Coqual) found that executive presence accounts for 26 percent of what it takes for an individual to get promoted. A Harvard Business Review survey study found that 52 percent of men and 45 percent of women said being perceived as having executive presence was more important to being promoted than having any other specific qualification. And (here we go again) several studies have found that developing executive presence was one of the two top reasons executives received coaching.

A piece on executive presence, produced in 2023 by Management Consulted, included some examples that give the notion of "control" more specificity.

- "Sally is always attentive in meetings … She always remains calm during stressful conversations."
- "Cam stands tall with perfect posture … Cam speaks at just the right pace and at the right volume … His tone of voice grabs the attention of the room."
- "Lisa is always impeccably dressed and on time to meetings … She looks people in the eyes as she speaks to them and listens attentively."

What Executive Presence Is All About: Control

In "Executive Presence: A Model of Highly Effective Leadership," consultants at Bates wrote:

> *We conducted the first, science-based research into executive presence to uncover specific behaviors behind what people mean by executive presence. The results of our research led us to build a leadership model and assessment, the Bates Executive Presence Index.*

The report went on to say:

> *"Several studies have found that developing executive pres-*
> *ence was one of the top two reasons executives received*
> *coaching. Yet, when we first began to research execu-*
> *tive presence in 2011, there was no clear definition of it.*
> *While senior executives would say they want their lead-*
> *ers to have 'it,' they could not tell you exactly what they*
> *were looking for."*
>
> *—(Bates 2021)*

With all due respect, I can confidently report that what they were looking for is CONTROL.

Now, here's how I want to explain the notion of "control." You are going to see, as you continue to read, that the global leaders I interviewed for this book observed "executive presence" in young people who caught their eye, and the young people in question revealed this presence quality through an unusual level of CONTROL. I'm going to make the case that in looking at this from a strategic level, executive presence is all about control. Control over messaging, control over body language, and control over project oversight.

Think of this on a continuum from absolute control to out of control. An argument with someone, private or public, can reveal this to you. In many dramas—movies, TV, or stage plays, for example—the actors skillfully portray a continuum of control. One example, and please YouTube this if you don't remember seeing it, is *The Godfather*. The movie opens with a character asking the Godfather (Marlon Brando as Don Corleone) to punish some boys who hurt his daughter. Don Corleone listens with the only movement being his hand slowly petting a cat. When he begins speaking, pay attention to the total absence of movement. It signals power. His body stays totally still, and his words are delivered slowly.

Is it an example of executive presence? Yes. To an extreme. (It's worth noting that he wears a tuxedo in the scene. Another sign of presence in appearance. I will talk more about appearance as we move forward.)

Then at one point, Brando stands. That breaks the freeze he created by just sitting. It's very much like a training film on body language, and it is used effectively.

And since we're focusing here on the beginning of a career and being spotted early as a highflier, in *The Godfather Part II*, Don Corleone is played by Robert DeNiro as a young guy. There's a scene with him sitting behind a desk and listening to a man who has come to apologize. He, again, just sits without movement and listens with searing eye contact on the speaker. Then he abruptly sits up to shake hands and breaks the "freeze," you could say. He became more friendly.

People trained as I was trained are very much like a film director. If I thought my client needed advice on how to show executive presence, it's like me to say, "Sit down in the boardroom. Sit straight. Keep your hands on the table. Slow down your pace. Look at the board members. Begin your opening, which you have thought about and prepared the previous day."

To conclude this little lesson on acting, whenever seminar participants ask me how to continue to hone their skills after a seminar, I have always said, "Keep your eyes and ears open for how people are portrayed in popular culture. Read novels that feature leaders. Watch movies and TV shows that do the same. Remember the adage 'a genius looks at what everyone might look at but sees what few people see.'" That is a righteous TNT!

There's another "real-life" scenario where many readers have experienced control or have seen executive presence being demonstrated. I'm going to call it "Parental Presence." I have often told my clients that the books on parenting and the books on leadership are remarkably similar. After Stephen Covey wrote *The 7 Habits of Highly Effective People*, there were a number of follow-up titles including Daniel Huerta's *Seven Traits of Effective Parenting* and Sean Covey's *The 7 Habits of Highly Effective Teens* as well as other similar publications. You will see the notion of presence in all of them. I guarantee you, when a parent has a serious and heart-to-heart talk with a teen at home, the instinct to show control and confidence emerges without a consultant nearby.

On the opposite end of the spectrum: If you watch a movie scene or a live interaction with people yelling at each other, look for an absence of body control. Arms and hands start flying. Volume can go sky high. Words can come tumbling out, as I describe it in this book's introduction, like a drum solo. Eventually, the "fighters" calm down. Maybe even sit down. One says to the other, "Let's just sit and quietly talk this out." That's a sign of someone wanting to inject control over the interaction.

There's no executive presence in yelling or waving arms around. That doesn't mean that executives may not wave their arms around from time to time. They are as likely to lose control as anyone. But they know it's not showing their best self. Anyone sitting on a board watching such a thing would have serious qualms about an executive's leadership.

Delving into Decisiveness

So how do you, as you embark on your career, show an already developed sense of presence (which I like calling "a presence in the room") by exerting some control? Turning again to more scientifically grounded studies, one conducted by Thrive Street Advisors surveyed 268 senior executives who brought the term "gravitas" into the conversation. I've heard this term used many, many times by folks who have reached out to our firm, CDA, for seminars or coaching. As I mention earlier in this chapter, Thrive Street reported that 67 percent of the people surveyed said "…gravitas is what really matters." (Hewlett 2024) They also reported that "signaling that 'you know your stuff cold,' that you can go 'six questions deep' in your domains of knowledge, is more salient than either communication … or appearance."

Even though the executives used intellectual power when they brought gravitas into the equation, the fact is this quality of gravitas implies a dignity or seriousness of manner. So you can't divorce communication skill from the overall perception. Once again, "seriousness of manner" is another way to describe control over the message and the style that goes with it.

Other quotes from their surveyed executives included things like this: "In a crisis, you can lean into the wind, acknowledge your shortcomings, and rise above them; or you can take cover. You can acquire gravitas, the cornerstone of a real leader."

In addition, they reported that "being able to make decisions isn't so much the issue as needing to appear decisive in public— the difference again, between doing the job of a leader and *looking* like one as you're doing it, between demonstrating competence and exuding *presence*."

When it comes to "appearing decisive in public," nothing is quite as important as what I am about to describe. I want to show you the difference between the settings you are thought to be prepared to talk about, like a PowerPoint presentation (sometimes called "a set piece"), and those that require thinking on your feet. I call the former the "proacting parts of the day," and the latter the "reacting parts." I use the term *proacting* because you've had a chance to prepare in advance and everyone knows that. Compare that to the *reacting* experiences where you are thinking on your feet. Sometimes people describe certain questions as "coming out of left field." Those require reacting skills. And the reacting skill that is most clearly demonstrated and required of you is, as referred to earlier, decisiveness.

Reacting is shown primarily in the way you answer questions and the way you respond to challenges, as you find out in the following sections.

Questions

Questions you are asked, in a meeting with other team members, which seem to be seeking a yes or no answer are the ones that offer a chance to be seen as decisive. These questions, which people have come to call "closed-ended questions," have been given short shrift by experts who teach interviewing. Those experts argue that these questions don't give the responder an opportunity to be more "open" in the answer.

The fact, however, is that the questioner doesn't want a long open-ended response. They want a short answer that responds directly to the choice they want you to make. There are only three choices available to you: "yes" or "no" or "I don't know."

If you are asked by the Senior Vice President of Marketing, "Do you think we need to bring a consultant in to help us?" the Senior VP does not want a lecture on the use of outside consultants. What they want is, "Yes. It's exactly what we need right now," or "No. We're not ready for that at this point," or "I don't know, but I can research the question and get back to you" or "I don't know, so I'd like to survey the rest of the team first."

On the technical side, it's a way to show you are listening to the question. But on the strategic, long-term reputation you build, it's a way to show you are decisive, that you can choose to be decisive, and you can do it in public.

If I had a dollar for every time someone asked me to work with another person about "getting to the point" answering questions, I could buy a house on Maui. How many times has someone said to me, "I asked him what time it is, and I was told how to make a watch." For the asker, it's a matter of trying to get clarity on a topic from the responder. For the responder, though, it's a way to show decisiveness under pressure and by extension, executive presence. I am not saying that this is the only way leaders show decisiveness. But if communication has a place in the equation, it can become a major factor. Here's a TNT for you: One of the qualities of "yes" or "no" questions an asker can use, intentionally or not, is to add an "n't" to the word "do." For example, instead of "Do you think we need to bring a consultant in to help us?" the wording will be, "Don't you think we need to bring a consultant in to help us?" That small change can throw you off your game and cause you to lose your composure and probably make you feel defensive. Even though you would have said "no" if asked as "Do you think..." you will wonder what the consequences of your answer might be in the other version. A more senior asker saying, "Don't you think we need to bring a consultant in?" seems to be making a statement and not a question. But keeping your executive composure requires you to respond with some level of confidence as you say, "No. Not at this point," if that is your sincere feeling about it. Two sides require consideration.

Here is the thing: Either we give advice to the asker to ask easier questions in order to be less "aggressive," or we give advice to the person taking the question on how to stay composed under pressure. I have a bias toward the latter because that is how I was trained. I will say, however, that if I were giving tips to the aggressive question asker because there was feedback about aggressiveness, I would have advised the asker to be more judicious in the use of the leading questions—the ones with the "n't"—because they do not sound like real questions. They sound like opinions and that is tougher to handle for the responder.

Did you know that in the law, you can only ask leading questions in specific situations like cross-examination? Watch *Law and Order* one evening. You'll hear an attorney say, "Objection. Leading the witness," if the question is something like "Shouldn't you have said something?" instead of "Should you have said something?"

Challenges

Maintaining presence while taking challenges instead of questions is a little different situation. Challenges are not put in question form. They are statements of opinion. A question, again, could be "Should we move our manufacturing facility to another location?" A challenge, however, is worded more like, "It seems to me we should move our manufacturing facility to another location."

My suggestion to you is to respond by saying, "I hear you. It's been suggested by several people. I'm still of the opinion that we stay put for a while longer."

This TNT is called "Feel, Felt, and Found." The classic statement would have been "I understand how you feel. I think others here have felt the same way. However, we have found, etc., etc."

There's an interesting behavior I've observed that covers two issues at the same time. It's the phenomenon of the vocalized pause "uhhhh." I think this is the right place to give you a TNT about that. The reason your executive presence and decisiveness quotient, you could say, are both at risk here is the placement of the "uhhhh." The "uhhhh" has a habit of showing up just before the most important part of your thought: the direct object of the sentence. When you react with an "uhhhh," it makes the listener question your courage to make your point in a strong fashion. Ergo, you don't sound as decisive.

Here is an example:

> *"Brie said, 'The reason I'm concerned about this is it risks our reputation.'"*

Now look at it this way:

> *"Brie said, 'The reason I'm concerned about this is it risks our ... uhhhh ... reputation.'"*

Of all the places to vocalize a pause, this is the worst. Had there been nothing but a silent pause, the listeners are actually so attuned to what you are about to say it's as if they are hanging on each word. Stop right now and say it out loud. You'll notice what I'm describing immediately.

Your reputation for executive presence, which is not as important as your reputation for decisiveness but certainly worth improving on, comes into play for the reason cited earlier: lack of this presence makes your message sound out of control, and that implies to the listener(s) that your thinking may also be out of control.

So, while we are on this subject, I'm going to give you the most profound TNT about vocalized pausing you will ever read. Instead of beating yourself up and looking for ways to stop saying it, or putting a dollar in a jar every time you say it (sorry, Toastmasters, maybe it's still a quarter), tell yourself there's something to start doing and not something to stop doing. You have to say to yourself, "I am going to start and stop a beautiful short sentence."

Here's that example again: "The reason I am concerned about this is it risks our reputation." There. Easy-peasy. Well, okay, it might take some practice, but oh my, is it ever worth it.

Winston Churchill was quoted as saying, "I got into my bones the essential structure of the ordinary British sentence, which is a noble thing." That thought, the nobility of the ordinary British sentence, sends chills up the spine of anyone who has a belief about how important great communication can and should be.

While we're on the topic of communication, here's something else Churchill said: "Of all the talents bestowed upon men, none is so precious as the gift of oratory. He who enjoys it wields a power more durable than that of a great king." (I am going to forgive Churchill for an egregious use of the male pronoun. It was the times.) However, I do not think Churchill meant to focus on stand-up speaking exclusively. So much of what was said in his lifetime was said into a microphone for radio listeners or at a meeting with business tycoons. But the spirit holds: speaking well can bring you so much satisfaction.

If your sentences were short and sweet, you would avoid the second most troublesome appearance of "uhhh." Check this out first: "I loved every minute of it." Noble. Churchill would have said to you, "Well said."

Now this way: "I loved every minute of it and, uhhh, I can't wait to do it again but, uhhh, I may not get the chance." If you say "and," "but," or "so" you will be on the verge of a vocalized pause. Such pauses are totally unnecessary. Without them you have, "I loved every minute of it. I can't wait to do it again. I may not get the chance." Hemingway would have said, "Well said." If you insist on those three conjunctions, I can't stop you. I am simply telling you that you are on the verge every time of "uhhh."

The Delivery of a Message

Jeff Weiss of the Center for Corporate Innovation said this about executive presence in an interview with me:

> *"I don't often have the opportunity to observe people in a business setting at the start of their career. I want to describe someone I saw who has all the qualities you are interested in, but I saw him later in his career. I was told by others in our firm that he exuded these traits early and they contributed to his later success. He is CMO, a Chief Medical Officer.*

The first thing I noticed about him was his physical presence. He had composure and charisma. He is tall, strikingly handsome, dressed very conservatively and in good shape. Everything was tucked in, and the tie was just right. When he spoke, he put his thoughts in strategic perspective and in a very simple way. I have to say he was not telling us something new. It was just so well put. It was concise and his body language was consistent with the words. The volume and pacing made me believe and there was such an energy behind it so that he made me, and others in the room, believe it and believe that it was important. He said, "It hasn't been done yet. And it will be difficult to do. And we need to be committed to it." It's amazing that I remember the message so well as a result of how it was delivered."

Jeff went on to say that so often he's thought about whether the message or the way a message is delivered is of prime importance. In this instance the way it was delivered made the message resonate. "You can't have one without the other," he concluded.

In Just a Few Words

I want to turn now to an interview with Bob Azelby. Bob is an experienced Chief Executive Officer and veteran board member who has spent more than 30 years in the biopharmaceutical industry.

He served as President and Chief Executive Officer of Eliem Therapeutics, Inc., from October 2020 to February 2023. Bob was the Chief Commercial Officer of Juno Therapeutics for three years. He spent 15 years in commercial roles at Amgen, Inc. He holds a BA in Economics and Religious Studies from the University of Virginia and an MBA from Harvard Business School.

Here's what Bob said as a description of "presence" in the face of senior executives when one woman was at the start of her career.

"I want to focus on a lady without mentioning her name. I suspect she'll know I am talking about her if she reads The Highflier Handbook. I was in a board meeting. The company in question is valued at 15 to 20 billion; I'm fortunate to be on that board. I was part of a discussion with HR folks and about HR. The HR executive after listening to a presenter said, 'We like this person but we do not think she has the 'it' factor.' She said, 'You just know it when you see it.' And I agree with that comment. How do you put on the bones of the effect? It's not that easy. This is such a great topic. I was involved in a meeting/presentation which included some people from an MBA program who had a chance to make an impression with senior executives. These folks come in, do six months, rotate into different areas of commerce, and then they get a full-time job. She was seen as a high-energy person.

In another case, I would describe someone else as high IQ, tough as nails and the ability to work cross-functionally. She asked a lot of questions. And I would say the biggest factor was a command of the audience. And I have seen a million presentations. Here's what really stood out to me. She said something that made me sit back and think 'Wow, that was impressive and unexpected.'

We were going to launch a product. It was for a form of leukemia. It's a blood disorder. It strikes more males than females and they are often in their 40s, in the prime of life. She was describing the patient and the physician. She was asked, 'If you were to describe the patient in a word or two, how would you describe them?' It was a huge presentation.

She said, 'The words I would use are pissed off.' *As potentially inappropriate as that phrase is in the culture, she said
it. It was edgy. But think about it. These are 40-year-old
dudes, maybe married and with kids. Now they have a
disease. It could kill them. She captured it perfectly. That
solidified her to me as WOW. This is a young person early
in her career and she just nailed it. She had the confidence
and presence to do it."*

You know we're getting at executive presence immediately when
you hear the word *command*.

Here executive presence is embodied in the ability to reduce a
complex answer to two words. That talent, that ability to express
something so potentially heavy with feelings into two words, is worth
your effort to think about and practice. I prize one-syllable English. It
had that. I prize the risk taking, when it seems to be appropriate, that
she invoked in that meeting. It's a phrase that the senior executives
in the room had used a million times in their lives and she touched
a nerve, a positive nerve of similarity with their feelings about such
a condition, when she said it. It was as if she had said, "What would
your feelings have been if it were you?" She scored on presence in a
meeting full of senior executives and she scored as a person willing
to go for it. Bob was certainly impressed.

Showing Multidimensional Personality

Here's yet another critical TNT. I would want someone talking about
you, describing your "personality" to someone else, to express the
notion that you are a multidimensional person and not a one-trick
pony, so to speak. Maybe the wording would be something like this:
"She has a remarkable ability to connect with people where they are.
But she is careful, strategic you might say, in how often she invokes

the edgy quality you saw today. You can't take today as an illustration of her full personality. But when it's needed, she has it."

Bob also spoke to me about someone who, unfortunately, did not get the multidimensional description. He said, "Another person is a guy who is also smart. Harvard Business School. Tall, imposing. Analytical out the wazoo. If he gets a project, he'll tear into it and break it apart. But he's a little soft. Too nice. Too polite. He doesn't have that other dimension. The hard side."

So there you have it. To address something in your manner and style that is perceived to be important for you as a highflier, you do not need to show that quality all the time. You have to show enough to qualify you, so to speak, as a well-rounded contributor: "You will find him soft in some situations. But make no mistake, I have seen his hard side too."

The Power of Charisma

One last concept fits in this chapter. It is the notion of charisma. I was reminded about it once again, because it has come up a million times in my career, when a piece appeared in *The Wall Street Journal* entitled "Is 'Rizz' the Secret to Getting Ahead at Work?" Rachel Feintzeig opened the piece with this:

> *"Great leaders have it. Gen Z has a new word for it. Can the rest of us learn it? Charisma—or rizz, as current teenage slang has anointed it—can feel like an ephemeral gift some are just born with. The chosen among us network and chit-chat, exuding warmth as they effortlessly hold court. Then there's everyone else, agonizing over exclamation points in email drafts and internally replaying the joke they made in the meeting, wondering if it hit."*
>
> *—(Feintzeig 2024)*

I encourage you to read the full article. Here is a top line notion I want to call your attention to here and will again throughout this book. Feintzeig wrote, "At its heart, charisma isn't about some grand performance. It's a state we elicit in other people ... It's about fostering connection and making our conversation partners feel they are charming—or interesting or funny—ones. The key is to ask deeper, though not prying, questions that invite meaningful and revealing responses ... And match the other person's vibes."

Think about this: charisma and charming and character all begin with "char," and all of them have listening at the heart of the definition. You show how great a listener you are in the responses to questions you ask or statements you make. That last line, "questions you ask or statements you make," describes the day for all of us.

Socrates spoke about questions and their power. Aristotle described the power of great statements. Think of it this way: When you ask questions you are invoking the "Socratic" method, so to speak. When you make statements, you are living proof of Aristotle. How is that for rhetorical theory in a nutshell? It's one of my favorite TNTs.

Chapter 3

Your Strategic Mind

I noticed early how brilliant they were.

I must admit I have had a special interest in the entire notion of "strategic" since I began my practice. The comment "he or she is a strategic thinker" is as big a compliment about someone's competence as "well put together" is about someone's appearance.

I have a hypothesis about "a strategic mindset" and we will see if you agree. Here it is: The level of executive I have had the pleasure to meet and work with must have had a strategic mind or they would not have reached the level they have reached. Here's a list of titles most of my clients have: CEO, CFO, CCO, CPO, COO, EVP, VP, Director, Controller, or Senior Manager.

While I believe many of them have this "strategic mindset," it is also true that they do not always "talk the talk" of it or write in a way that shows it. And that is a shame. Any quality you have but do not show in words is just a shame. I have been a banshee for clients about saying things that show a quality I know they possess. And not all of them were described to me by their colleagues as demonstrating a strategic mind.

In this chapter, I describe the differences between showing your tactical and strategic thinking ability, depending on the situations you face and the people you are talking with. It is important you be recognized for both perspectives.

Be Strategic *and* Tactical in Meetings

I applaud the effort for big-picture thinking; however, do not let it obscure your knowledge of critical detail. That quality in you is typically called your *tactical* side.

Here is an example of how you would show both your strategic mindset and your tactical side in a meeting. Let's say you first said, "The overall message here is that the summer travel boom is failing to benefit airlines worldwide." That is an example of a strategic takeaway presumably from your analysis of data.

Next you would say, "One reason is the cost of a barrel of oil. It is hovering around $80. Before the pandemic is was $55 a barrel. Another reason is unit cost. We forecasted that a unit cost excluding fuel would fall from 6.7 cents to 5.7 cents. Instead, it is expected to rise to 7.3 cents."

Imagine being in a meeting and bringing both the strategic conclusion and the tactical numbers to the table. There will be positive reactions about both the depth of your knowledge and the quality of your conclusion. The compliment I want my clients and all my readers to get is this: "They have remarkable strategic vision. But make no mistake they are just as good at detail. It just depends on the situation." In fact my favorite compliment about a client from a few years ago was, "He knows retail at the subatomic level. Hell, at the particle level."

Strategy Sessions Are Good for You and the Organization

Here's the research. In 2013, Polboon Nuntamanop, Ilkka Kauranen, and Barbara Igel published a study in the *Journal of Strategy and Management* titled "A New Model of Strategic Thinking Competency." The stated purpose was to offer "new insights into strategic thinking, proposing a model of strategic thinking competency." The authors were guided by the belief that strategic thinking plays a role in corporate profitability and output. They cite a study by McAdam and Bailie (2002) that confirmed this belief. They also cited a study by Kraus, Harms, and Schwarz (2006) that concluded that strategic planning in even small firms contributed to the growth of the firm.

But look at this quotation from the article: "Despite a wide consensus on the importance of strategic thinking to business performance, an extensive literature review has found few studies that define what strategic thinking is or empirically verify how strategies and strategic actions business leaders in practice take relate to strategic thinking." Does this sound familiar? It's remarkably like the definition of leadership that Jacob Morgan wrote about, and I cited at the beginning of Chapter 1. None of the leaders could define it.

Strategic Messaging and Tactical Messaging Are Different

I want, at this point, to clearly distinguish your tactical messaging from your strategic messaging.

If you are thought of as an "SME," or a subject matter expert, you are going to be asked for your view on the topics people expect you to be familiar with. If you think of the basic logical layout of information, spoken or written, it's a progression from a general statement to specific examples, or it's turned on its head and goes from examples to a general statement.

If you lead tactically, the first information your listeners will hear typically includes data. You will then give your interpretation of that data and finally suggest a direction that you think offers a positive outcome or future. Since your conclusion is the last thing your listeners hear, they are likely to remember your sense of *strategic* direction.

If you lead strategically, your listeners will hear your suggestion followed by the analysis that led up to it followed by the data. That approach will highlight your familiarity with and depth on the topic. And that highlights your *tactical* skill.

Maybe the reason organizations do not organize tactical thinking seminars is the belief that there's plenty of that to go around. Maybe too much. As I wrote in this book's preface, I am thrilled that my client is you, the reader, and not the organization you work for. I am not trying to encourage strategic planning exercises for a company. I am trying to instill the role *your* communication, the messages *you* speak and write, plays in the perception that you are a strategic thinker. And that is primarily because it comes up so much in my work when I ask for feedback about someone I am going to advise: "He or she needs to work on their strategic thinking and vision."

Either the organization offers strategic planning as a company exercise at which executives participate in the hope that each person will benefit, or the organization offers strategic thinking as a seminar or individualized "coaching" in the hope that the larger entity benefits. I am a true believer in the second option although, of course, the organization could do both. If the participants in a strategic planning weekend exercise were all better at strategic thinking, believe me, the outcome would be significantly better.

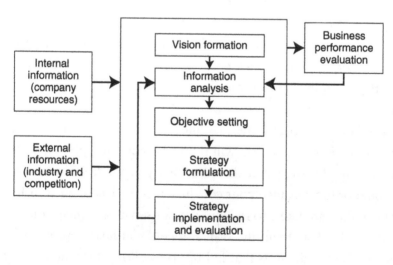

Figure 3.1 Your ideas could be added at any point during this process. *Source*: © John Wiley & Sons, Inc.

Figure 3.1 shows you a process for typical strategic planning programs. This process was referred to in the article by Nuntamanop, Kauranen, and Igel cited earlier.

I have participated in a number of strategic planning offsites for corporate offices throughout my career. The process is very similar across all the vendors who facilitate them. If you were there, you would have a chance to contribute to an early discussion of the group's current situation—the strengths and weaknesses. All of that would be recorded and distributed later. The group would then start brainstorming about where it hopes to go—the visioning exercise. Soon after, there would be a conversation about priorities and listing them in order of importance. There is often an acronym, SMART, to guide that conversation. The goals should be "specific" and "measurable" (that's S and M). Following that, the group would talk about potential blocks to getting the work done. Finally, there's the action plan and a strategy for getting the result out to all stakeholders in the organization in order for everyone to be what has come to be called "aligned."

So the TNT of that looks something like this. Think of yourself as a character in a book. A book that took the reader inside a strategic planning meeting. You would want to come across as a strategic thinker as well as a clear communicator. Others in the room would be listening to you attentively. Here are your potential lines: (You are Corey)

> Corey said, "I see us at the end of next year having acquired two companies that will propel our growth. That's my vision."_____ said, "What data do you have to support that?"
>
> Corey said, "Turn to page 5 in your deck. You'll see it all."
>
> _____ chimed in and said, "Let's go around the table and set objectives."

Corey said, "I have some thoughts on the three biggest ones. Those are revenue enhancement, quick entry into the market, and a smooth transition."

In this book, I am going to show you other frameworks for talking like a strategic thinker. The one I have just shown you is a great start.

Adding Tactical Tips to Your Strategic Messaging

In the same 2013 article by Polboon Nuntamanop, Ilkka Kauranen, and Barbara Igel that I mention earlier, they speak to *strategic thinking*. Are you ready? "A common definition of strategic thinking in terms of its characteristics is not found. Hanford (1995) suggests that the ability to think strategically requires developing of: thinking concepts, thinking skills, thinking styles, and thinking techniques."

In my view, the first thing you must do is speak in a way that comes across as strategic thinking. In other words, how does anyone know if you are a strategic thinker unless you speak in a way that "markets" that quality? I need to show you more research on this and then will come back to more TNTs. Do not skip to that now. The science is too interesting to skip.

Research on Strategic Thinking

In a chapter titled "Strategic Communication Requires Strategic Thinking" (in the book *Strategic Communication in Context: Theoretical Debates and Applied Research*), Peggy Simcic Bronn says ... "that to be successful, strategic communication needs leaders who are strategic thinkers and who take a systems approach."

In the *International Journal of Strategic Communication* (Hallahan et al. 2007), the case is made that strategic communication is "the purposeful use of communication by an organization to fulfill its mission."

I am going to pause right here to remind you that a highflier uses strategic messaging to enhance the work of the organization and to enhance his or her reputation as a competent colleague. In fact, Zerfass, Vercic et al. (2018) remind their readers that to be a part of strategic decision making, executives need to exhibit strategic thinking competency: "Strategic communication encompasses all communication that is substantial for the survival and sustained success of an entity. Specifically, strategic communication is the purposeful use of communication by an organization or other entity to engage in conversations of strategic significance to its goals." That is an ever more important reason to put your effort into learning the skill of talking and writing like someone who is a candidate for a team that exhibits this competency.

I want to remind you here of something I said in the preface. In my world (hopefully our world now), the individual is the unit of analysis. That's you. There is every reason to improve your strategic thinking reputation related to how it helps your organization. Zerfass, Vercic et al. write that strategic thinking and planning contributes to the sustained success of the organization you work for. But this book is primarily, if not solely, focused on you and the benefit of talking and writing as a strategic thinker to enhance your reputation.

Showing Strategic Thinking with Features and Benefits

At this point I'll offer up one of the simplest ways to show strategic thinking.

Salespeople are taught early on in their training about the difference between a feature and a benefit of their product. They are encouraged to "sell the benefits." Elmer Wheeler wrote a book called *How I Mastered My Fear of Public Speaking* in which he introduced the idea of "don't sell the steak, sell the sizzle."

We do not call corporate influence skills "selling." But there are parallels. The *benefits* are the same as *strategies*, whether in a corporate presentation or simply sitting in a meeting and expressing your opinions. *Features* are to *tactics* as *benefits* are to *strategies*. That is exactly how you should think of it.

All executives start thinking about your ideas and their first question is "why." That question is generally seeking the *benefit* of your idea. Will it contribute to revenue? Will it shorten the time between deploying and realizing the benefit? Will it be seen as a positive move by our investors?

So, let's think about this notion as bringing forth an idea at an executive presentation and how important it is that you sell the sizzle, the benefit, the strategic value of your idea and, by extension, your strategic thinking. Close your eyes and imagine yourself starting your PowerPoint presentation. You are there to suggest a move. You think the company should move the manufacturing plant to another location. You start speaking:

We are here today to suggest we move our manufacturing facility to another state. Take a look at this slide for some powerful data. Here are the costs we expect to see in construction. Here are the predicted taxes we see. Here is some data on the employee base. You can see it's a highly educated workforce.

These are the *features*. They are *tactical* ideas, the details, the numbers.

You conclude your presentation with this:

In review, the construction costs are significantly lower than you might expect so we will save a considerable amount of money. Our stockholders are going to be thrilled to hear that. The tax base is so low it will benefit us financially almost as much or more as introducing our newest approved drug. Once again, a savings that our stockholders will find very appealing. There is a large pool of educated people in that state who will be highly motivated and energized to work with us long into the future. We can be optimistic about our future there.

All of those are *benefits*. They are the illustration of your strategic thinking. When it's over, and people talk a few hours later at a company happy hour, when your name comes up someone will say, "That was a great presentation. It was so powerful. And I was impressed with the strategic thinking, the big idea thinking, that went into it."

A Real-Life Example

I always like telling my clients to learn more about communication by looking and listening to what they experience in daily life. If you begin looking into buying an electric vehicle, for instance, study the sales literature and the salesperson for the messaging. Here's what one website says about its vehicles' features.

Engineered with an all-electric architecture ... vehicles provide a very low probability of rollover risk and occupant injury ... Eight cameras and powerful vision processing provide 360 degrees of visibility, detecting nearby objects like pedestrians, bicyclists and vehicles.

A trained salesperson would say to you, "This car is engineered with an all-electric architecture. And for you the driver, that means no visits to the dealer servicing your typical issues with combustion engines which you know are costly and take time. You save money and you save your valuable time." Those are the benefits … saving money and time and trouble.

He or she then says, "There is a low probability of rollover risk and occupant injury. That means you have a continual feeling that your family will be safe and sound with you at the wheel." Again, that's a benefit.

Continuing, your friendly salesperson says: "The car features eight cameras and powerful vision processing providing 360 degrees of visibility, detecting nearby objects like pedestrians, bicyclists and vehicles. That again means you can drive stress free from the fear of being involved in accidents. You won't be calling your insurance company and trading information with other drivers as you would with combustion engine cars. It's not guaranteed but the chances are significantly lower."

Once again, the benefits. The strategy, if you will, leads to buying such a car.

A Balancing Act: Avoiding Too Much Time on Tactics

Finding a balance between strategy and tactics is crucial. If you spend too much time on tactics, you will be described as tactical, not strategic. I want the people who describe you to say, "They are responsibly detailed, both tactical and strategic. They really get it! They are remarkably knowledgeable about the detail."

What I am about to say may annoy some of you, but the emphasis on fixing things or getting things done can lead to the description

"He or she is an individual contributor." The argument that is made about this phenomenon of being pigeonholed as not having leadership skills comes from a reputation of knowing how to do things: creating budgets, enforcing policies, and carrying out procedures. Today being a manager (that's the title you would get) is not as important as being a leader (Katzenbach 1996).

Peggy Simcic Bronn writes that strategy is a practice "concerned with the overall performance of a system ... Strategy implies a high-level perspective, a broader scope, and greater responsibility that contrasts with the tactical or operational levels of the firm." (Bronn 2021) She goes on to say that it's "about planning based on long-term goals and objectives ... acting and allocating resources to achieve goals and objectives. Strategies determine courses of action and should address how to gain and sustain advantage over competitors, all in a dynamic and changing business environment."

I want you, my reader, where my primary interest lies, to have this said of you in your annual performance review: "They speak to and write about planning based on goals and objectives that they've set as a team. They allocate funds and people, whatever is necessary, to achieve those. They talk about what we need to do to sustain our competitive advantage over competitors ... all in an environment of constant change. They truly get it." That is the ultimate compliment about competence. It was because you showed strategic thinking. That is what I want for all highfliers!

Title, Agenda, Result

Warren Keith Schilit wrote that the way middle-level managers potentially influence their superiors in strategic decision making is to present ideas through rational or persuasive arguments (Schilit 1990). Continuing in this vein, M. Reza Vaghefi and Alan B. Huellmantel, in their book *Strategic Management for the XXIst Century*, found that at the senior manager leadership level, which they defined as directors, vice presidents, and executive vice presidents, 70 percent of the skills needed were strategic-conceptual and entrepreneurial. They defined those as strategic thinking, scenario planning, and issues management.

TNT time: Assuming Schilit is right, that managers influence their superiors in strategic decision making through persuasive argument, the communication technique for "rational or persuasive arguments" involves a building of a presentation from top down or bottom up, depending on your guess as to what the listener likes. This then is not just a tip on how to be a good presenter, it's a tip about messages that come across to the listener as evidence of strategic thinking. The old saw has always been "tailor your message to the audience."

First you collect your thoughts by using this framework: T.A.R. T stands for title. The A stands for agenda and R stands for result. Sit at your computer and begin filling in the blanks so to speak. Here's an example:

- Today I will lay out three options for you to consider. (title)

- I will begin with some background of our investigation into the value of each option. Then I will lay each one out. Finally, I will focus on the one our team prefers. (agenda)

- We hope as a result of this discussion, you will be confident that we have selected the best possible choice as we move forward. (result)

"Traditional" Versus Strategic Thinking

Another interesting study by Barry Richmond included the notion that "strategic thinking" is a difficult abstraction. The question is this:

While it is easy to report on characteristics that describe a strategic thinker, can one learn to become a strategic thinker? (Richmond 1997). He lays out two columns that compare traditional thinking with strategic thinking. For example, he writes that traditionally, to understand the pieces that are a part of the whole, one must drill down into the details. In strategic thinking, you have a grasp of the details and you know how they are intertwined. Yet you have to be able to stand back from the detail, the trees, so to speak, so as to see the proverbial forest.

So, looking at the contrast of traditional and strategic thinking, here's what I would want you to say in a meeting to show strategic thinking.

The TNT: I encourage you to say something like, "Today we'll talk less about each part of our model. You'll see them listed. I want to talk instead about how they work together to achieve the synergy we're after."

Surely, you'll have looked into the way the pieces would fit into the whole puzzle. I simply want to make sure you say it so that it's clear you studied it and thought about it and knew you needed to say it.

First Do, Then Become

I think this is a good place to explain the belief of John B. Watson and B.F. Skinner that attitude follows behavior. This last bit applies to all of what I write in this book and what I have spent my career talking about. I want you to be confident that "talking the talk" isn't simply talking for the sake of talking. Talking first produces the aspirational attitude you seek. In this case, strategic thinking. I will not and cannot describe all of Skinner's writing about this, but I will say the following.

John B. Watson first emphasized the importance of studying observable behavior and rejected the study of internal mental processes. Watson believed that all behavior is learned, and he aimed to explain how it could be understood and controlled. Skinner expanded on the work of Watson. This approach rejects the notion of analyzing emotions, thoughts, or consciousness, instead focusing solely on what can be directly observed and measured. The messaging I am suggesting with my TNTs are the observable behavior. In addition to showing the listeners you are a strategic thinker through your messaging, you will become a better strategic thinker as a result.

I want to assure you, as a behaviorist myself, that if you first act and speak as a strategic thinker, you will become one. It's not simply an act for its own sake. I want to make this clear because there is so much legitimacy in the commitment to authenticity. I do not want to leave you with the "take away" that learning communication technique, no matter what the impression is that we want to leave, is "all an act." The act will have a major impact on who you are. First do it. Then become it.

Purpose, Curiosity, and Tenacity

I had a terrific interview with Curtis Anderson of Nursa. Their website includes these words:

> *"Success isn't about securing investors or achieving rapid growth but rather the lasting impact we create on the problem we set out to solve: getting a nurse to the bedside of every patient in need."*

This line serves as a great example of strategic thinking. Can you see, referring to features and benefits (tactics and strategy), that securing investors is the tactic? "Getting a nurse to the bedside of every patient in need" is the strategy. Curtis isn't only, as you will see, going to talk about someone who impressed him. He demonstrates strategic thinking himself.

Curtis founded Nursa in 2019 after recognizing inefficiencies in the traditional nurse staffing agency model. His vision was to create a platform that directly connects healthcare facilities with qualified nurses for short-term staffing needs, eliminating intermediaries and improving transparency. Nursa was born to get more nurses to more patients and has grown to complete more than 3 million patient hours annually. The company now operates across the United States. Curtis also serves as a volunteer to several community organizations.

Here's what Curtis said about someone who impressed him.

"I interviewed a product manager. At the front end of the interview, I want to get an understanding of what matters most to a person. I will usually ask that in some version of the question. 'What's important to you about what comes next?' His particular answer was very simple. He said, 'I want to do good work with people who want to do great work.' And wow, the answer itself was right. I said, 'Talk to me about that. What and how has that manifested itself? How have you seen that in your life before? How do you know you've been on a team like that?' And he proceeded to describe a story where he landed as the second prod-uct manager on a team. He worked through a number of data-centered problems with peers, making both quanti-tative and qualitative decisions. They were decisions that were based on anecdotes, both of which he described in confidence. He then said, 'I just want to do that trip again.' There was so much humility and authenticity with which he addressed it. What became evident and clear to me was he wanted to do work. And anyone who speaks of just

labor, like sweat-inducing labor, with that degree of emotion, I'm ready to make a bet on them. We'll send him an offer tomorrow."

The TNT here is not just what Curtis said about success, it's about how the candidate described his aspiration. It was a big picture statement, "I want to do good work with people who want to do great work," followed by an anecdote. That is a strategy followed by tactics. If you were asked, "What's important to you?" that is how I encourage you to prepare your thinking in advance of a meeting where you know you'll be asked for your opinion on something.

I have a seminar where clients prepare what is called *A Talking Point* to answer questions about their point of view. The framework has four sentences. It's a TNT. Here they are:

- My take on that is…
- The reason I say that is…
- Going forward I want to…
- For example…

That framework takes the listener from big picture to your logic with the added spice of a statement about the future (also a strategic-minded statement) followed by specifics again. The full statement using the framework might be, "I want to do good work with great people. I say that because so much of my satisfaction is wrapped up in my work and in my relationships. Going forward I plan to meet with the team to talk about where they see us in six months. For instance, we'll gather anecdotes as well as metrics on current trends in healthcare." There may be 100 versions of that coming from 100 different people. But the sound of provocative thinking will be there.

Let Yourself Fly

Bob Brisco, CEO of Internet Brands, gave me a perfect example of noticing a highflier blossom after getting some feedback. Bob's bona fides are fully detailed in Chapter 5 so I will go directly to his anecdote about strategic mindset.

"There was a young business analyst who joined Internet Brands two or three years out of university with a business degree from a top business school. Her level of analysis and insight was way beyond her years. That was clear in the interview process and in the first engagements we put her on. But we had to pull it out of her. She was timid sharing her opinions. It took a lot of coaching to have her understand that she was a superior analyst and was closer to the information and was adding value with her insights. She needed to get over her reservation. I think she was concerned about being perceived as arrogant or out of place and therefore offensive. But the flip side of that is you continue to be perceived as an analyst and not the strategic thinker you are. You are not engaged to get full credit. She began to put that lesson to work in situations where she can demonstrate that type of leadership.

The takeaway here is a need to go beyond the reluctance to leave the comfort of data. It is easy to opine on a recommendation that is rooted in data. I find that some executives are reluctant to form an opinion that could be considered risky without an overwhelming amount of data underneath it. While you can make a mistake by getting to the wrong conclusion, more often than not, the bigger mistake is not venturing forth to a valid hypothesis based on limited data and allowing the aftermath of that to unfold. That aftermath may be getting more data and validating it or parlaying that insight into neighboring insights that changed the whole complexion of the solution space. If you do not set yourself free to consider the hypothesis in a nimble way but instead be down into proving out in real detail every piece of it, you will not allow yourself to fly."

The TNT: "Allowing yourself to fly" because you were tolerant of the ambiguity of not knowing every piece of data but instead spoke out with your hypothesis not only leads to the compliment about strategic thinking but extends to "capital L" Leadership.

They Never Say No

I want to use this last place in this chapter to write about what some would call the full partner of "a strategic mind." As referenced earlier, that is "a detail-oriented mind."

I spoke to Gerry Fay. At the time he was with Avnet. He is a board member now. He has a reputation and the record to back it up for creating value, driving revenue and profit growth, and developing innovative global supply chain, operations, distribution, and logistics strategies as an integral part of a company's competitive advantage. He has led large-scale, complex projects, global initiatives, acquisitions, and organizational integrations. Here is the story he told me about a highflier who he was so enthusiastic in describing.

"There was this woman … who had just transferred from our European business. I was initially impressed that this is a person who was willing to uproot herself and move across the world. I remember the first meeting that I had with her. The first thing that really impressed me about her was that she was a very clear communicator. She told me why she

came back to the United States. In addition, she was very detail oriented. I complimented her on her communication skill and asked her how she acquired it. She told me the first job she had was doing the weather at a local TV station. When I asked her what she wanted to do she said, 'I want to take over whatever is most screwed up and fix it.' Now, most people want to run away from that. I had kind of built my career doing the same thing, I kept getting put into situations where something was broken and asked to fix it. And I learned a lot from that."

I need to pause at this point to remind you of other TNTs I have previously written about. One, she was a *risk taker* willing to move to the United States. Two, she was a *clear communicator*. Three, and this is the point of the story, she was *detail oriented* and so is Gerry. Four, she was *a fixer*. (Parenthetically, I have suggested to all my clients over the years that it is a good idea to watch the weather person on their local TV station because they have terrific skill at what is essentially a PowerPoint presentation. Think about it.)

Now, back to Gerry.

"I assigned her an account that we had a bad relationship with. I told her, 'Okay, you want something screwed up? Here you go.' Through her detail mindset, totally data driven, she totally turned that account around. With her clear explanations, she was very good at telling the customer she would do whatever she could for them but also clear at drawing a line and using data to do it. She would say, 'This is why what you're asking me to do doesn't work. But based on what you want to do, maybe this is a way we could get there.' And she didn't just say 'no.' She brought solutions to the table for the customer. I was very impressed with that.

An opening came up for a better job and it was immediately offered to her. She did a fantastic job. She was somebody who you knew was going to go places. A few years later I told her, 'I want you to run our global supplier program.'"

"Allen," Gerry said to me, "Now she's a Senior Vice President at Google."

That, dear reader, is a great place to end this chapter.

Chapter 4

Character

The ones that have it are special.

Competence, executive presence, and strategic thinking—covered in earlier chapters—are so much easier to define than is character. But people still try. Michael Burgoon, whom I studied with at West Virginia University, wrote in his book *Human Communication* that "the popular rejoinder, 'You're a good man, Charlie Brown,' is a good way to look at character. It describes goodness, decency and trustworthiness."

Burgoon acknowledges that, even then, in the 1970s, people became skeptical about the character of our national leaders. Recently someone said to me about politicians, "They all lie." I reacted and said, "That is really cynical." He said, "Yes. But it's accurate." In any case, politicians have aimed a significant amount of time and money into strategies that put more stress on the character dimension of credibility. A lot of what they say, and project nonverbally, is to hope that they can change the image of trustworthiness coming from them to all of us who watch and listen to them.

In this chapter, you will see comments from interviewees and examples from studies to get a fuller grasp of what character means in the mind of those who appreciate it when they see it. When you read about the studies done on credibility, and review the qualities people look for in a credible person, they're often listed with the first three often called the "Big Three." Those are competence, composure, and character. But there is not an intention to list them in order of importance. To many of you, character will be uppermost in your mind depending on the person and the situation.

Studies on Character as a Part of Credibility

Just as I wrote about Aristotle and his layout of ethos, pathos, and logos in Chapter 1, character has been at the heart of studies on credibility. My old mentor from West Virginia University, Jim McCroskey, continued researching character and credibility long after I began my practice. I want to review just a smidgeon of it here.

Researchers have found competence and trustworthiness to predict credibility (McCroskey and Young 1981). In any election season, you can depend on people thinking about competence, character, and empathy to evaluate candidates. Donald Kinder (1986) wrote that competence and character, which he defines as honesty, trustworthiness, and even morality, are comparable to McCroskey's terms. People have studied character as a part of the credibility model to look at teachers, spouses, colleagues, public figures, employers, and even newscasters.

People who study politics have argued that competence has replaced character as the most important trait in the minds of voters (Funk 1997). What is especially interesting to me is that when research studies included people with high levels of political knowledge, they were even more likely to consider competence more than character (Funk 1997).

How about this research conclusion? In a study looking at the importance of character, the author suggested that President Bill Clinton's perceived leadership became more important than private character (Golden 1997). Steven Schneider (1996) argued in his commentary about the 1996 election that a cynical electorate "…no longer expects ethical behavior from a president but instead focuses on public performance." It is akin to asking, would you rather your brain surgeon be a lay person in your church who is devout or number one in his or her class at Stanford Medical School?

Character and Work Ethic

My personal take on character, based on literally thousands of phone calls and face-to-face meetings with executives to seek feedback on my clients, is that character has become a synonym for work ethic as well as showing respect for colleagues. Sometimes those two are intertwined. By intertwined I mean that showing a disciplined work ethic may be one of the ways you show respect.

The first interview I conducted to prepare to write this book was with Phil West. He is a partner at Steptoe in Washington, DC, and represents a variety of major corporations, domestic and foreign. He is considered one of the premier tax attorneys in the United States. He has had 40 years of experience, both public and private, including serving as International Tax Counsel for the United States Treasury Department. He has advocated before the IRS, the U.S. Congress, and several international organizations. He served as Steptoe's Chair from 2014 to 2021.

At this point, I need to tell you what my plan was from the start when it came to asking questions in the interviews I conducted in the "run up" to writing this book. I had no intention of asking "What qualities in a person do you consider leadership qualities?" There are just too many books and articles with that as the basis. My first question was, "Can you tell me about someone you saw early in their career, maybe at an informal meeting or presentation, who stood out from the crowd? Perhaps someone who you felt you would be keeping an eye on as a potential leader?" Here's how Phil responded:

"OK. One person comes to mind as we speak. There was something about the interpersonal interaction they showed that reflected a lack of awareness of how they came across. Maybe there was insufficient attention to the appropriateness of their style for the context in which they found themselves. Some people say, 'Young people are more casual, and they don't need to be as formal.' There are people who have left the firm and could be described as insufficiently sensitive to how they come across and its appropriateness to the context.

There's another quality I notice in people that I need to speak to as well. And quite a few people come to mind that I saw early in their career. There's an old aphorism that if you are not completely terrified, then you are not appropriately suited to the seriousness of the situation. One thing that can be a marker of someone who may not succeed is if they are not sufficiently paranoid. More particularly, if they aren't worried that they might make a mistake. What we do is very hard. You have to constantly be vigilant about making mistakes. You must be so attentive to detail."

In light of Phil's comments, I have a TNT. After a client meeting a few years ago, I sat down and constructed a framework called A Leader's Three Visions. I labeled them Farsight, Nearsight, and Insight.

- Farsight? That's obvious. The ability to visualize the possible future potential of ideas. And that quality is related to strategic thinking, which I discuss in Chapter 3.
- Nearsight is not so obvious. I defined it as your reputation for seeing the people close to you and recognizing their abilities …

talking with them and knowing things about them to give them the sense you care. Nearsight absolutely belongs in this chapter on character.

- I defined Insight as your ability to see inside yourself and let others know you do. That is, Phil says, "a person who knows how they come across and cares about it." I encourage you to say, out loud, "I know sometimes I can be a little abrupt with you. Please let me know when you experience that. I want to work on it." That is a TNT about knowing yourself.

What else do we take from Phil's comments? One is to pay close attention to the culture in which you work and strive to fit into it. Formal and informal is one of the markers. Formality or informality in dress. Formality and informality in the use of time. Formality and informality in how you write. I've been made aware for the last 15 years that experienced executives are bewildered at the low level of writing skill in younger employees. I am not going to outline examples of writing formality. But if we take just one of them, I will discourage you from using phonetic spellings in your emails. It's a scary thought that your informal spelling could be a clue into your character and a pleasant thought that adherence to the norms of proper spelling could be a clue, too—a positive one.

In addition, on the topic of being somewhat paranoid that you are not sufficiently worried about the worthiness of your work product, the TNT here is to express it in your messaging. If you are asked about a deadline, for instance, and whether you will make it on time, do not say, "Don't worry about it. All is well." The person who asked you about it expects that you are just as concerned as he or she is. I encourage you to say, "I am on top of it every moment. I know the pressure we are under to get this done on time."

A few years ago, I was in a meeting with a client named Bill Ashton. On this topic, the topic of caring about how well something is done, I remember an incident. His office had a glass wall. People could see him, and he could see people coming and going on the floor. At one point he said, "Let's take a quick break. I want to speak to the guy who just walked by the office." He called the fellow in, someone who reported to him, and asked about a deadline. The guy said, "Don't worry about it. It's not a big issue." When he walked out, Bill said, "I want you to take him on as a client. He does not understand that something I am worried about is something he, too, should be worried about." What does that tell you about paranoia, at least a legitimate concern, with deadlines and even more so when the person you report to is worried?

It is a pleasant thought to know that your attention to detail and concern about deadlines could be a clue about your character, too. It almost makes all the effort worthwhile.

The Heart of Authenticity

This is a fine spot to say something to you about your authentic self. *The Highflier Handbook*, being so full of tips, clearly asks you to add some behavioral options to your natural self.

I think of this issue as sociologists have thought about "nature and nurture" in parenting. Authentic is to nature as tips are to nurture. You may have given some thought to whether you are a product of nature or nurture or a combination. And most probably the latter. The thing that propels my energy level is the thought that I can help my client be a little more effective if the effort is directed at being a leader. In that way I am no different than a parent who wants his or her children to be successful. (To be clear: I do not think of my clients as children. Absolutely not!) But if I thought that deploying the tips you will read in this book will perhaps "round out" your natural self in the journey toward success at work, I would be so disappointed if I could not present them to you.

When I interviewed Roger Brossy, he spoke about authenticity before we began talking about a specific highflier. When I brought it up, he realized he had something to say about it. But first, a little about Roger: Roger Brossy has consulted with major corporations on executive compensation issues for 40 years. He co-founded Semler Brossy Consulting Group and serves as a member of the Dean's Council for New York University's Gallatin College.

Roger said, "I'm already rethinking the authenticity thing. I have another thought about it, which is that I am who I am. If in speaking to a group, I either out of insecurity or inflated ego or something else like that, try to make myself bigger than I am or more expert than I am, it's obviously going to make me inauthentic. So it may be that by employing your technology, what you are offering me is an opportunity to present who I really am in my best light and not need the crutch of bull…."

Now, back to Roger's anecdote about a highflier.

"The person I am thinking about had an innate curiosity that was so powerful, it overwhelmed their desire to look like they knew what we're talking about. They had lots of questions. They connected dots, they went off and looked things up on their own, brought those up in the conversation and challenged the status quo. They did not challenge it out of belligerence, but out of trying to figure out: Why is it this way? You know, why did they do that? Why do we do this kind of thing? And that to me is, like, number one. And sure, having a flair for the work or working hard, having sense of ownership over deadlines, wanting the work quality to stand on its own and be brilliant, intrinsically brilliant, not to win approval … someone else's approval, but just

to have it be great. On their own those are important. But I think the curiosity piece and the curiosity for a purpose, to understand the way things are and how much better they could be ... that is number one."

You can see the TNTs about authenticity practically jump out at you.

1. Ask questions without fretting about how insightful they make you sound. Just ask. At least have a bias toward asking.

2. Look things up on your own and bring them to the conversation.

3. Challenge the status quo. Say things like, "Here's the case I'd make for a different interpretation."

4. Pay attention to and deliver on deadlines.

Adhering to Deadlines and Time Commitments

Turning again to scientific research related directly to character, I want to focus on how much of your reputation as a highflier with character relates to how you use time. That category of nonverbal communication is called *chronemics* or the study of how we use our time. According to Michael Burgoon in his book *Human Communication*, "Our notions of time, how we use it, the timing of events, our emotional response to time, even the length of our pauses..." contribute to perceptions of us every day. We are so time conscious and there is so much meaning in the way we deal with time. That is precisely why I am going to devote space and time to how this underlies your character.

Think about this. We are obsessed with time, Burgoon writes. We can become disturbed, and this includes the people who are judging your character, if you "waste time" or do not realize and act upon the notion that "time is money."

Edward T. Hall in his book *The Silent Language* as, once again, quoted by Burgoon writes that for Americans, formal time is the "traditional, conscious time structure." Hall says we do not ever question the fact that time should be planned, and events must fit into a schedule. Results must be obtained in the foreseeable future. Promises to meet deadlines are taken very seriously. There are penalties for being late and not keeping commitments.

The positive spin on this research as far as TNTs are concerned is the terrific potential for compliments about character if you use the variable of time, chronemics, correctly.

- "I'll get it to you tomorrow morning."
- "I told them they had to get it to us tomorrow morning."
- "I was disappointed that he was late for the interview."
- "I answered the phone on the first ring."
- "I ended the meeting at exactly the time I committed to."
- "We have 15 minutes on the investor call. Let's not waste any of them."
- "The perception that we are more than capable of leading this effort is built on how we manage deadlines."

You may have always thought about how important time is. I encourage you to say it because your character is partially wrapped up in it. Communication is, at its heart, a marketing tool. It "markets" how you feel about things. It's the tree falling in the forest idea and whether it made a noise if no one was there to hear it.

Courage Shown in Speaking and Acting

I could have committed to writing an entire book on character based on all the words used to describe it. That, however, is not my goal in this chapter; rather, my goal is to make you aware of a few notions tied to character. The use of time and the paranoia about not making mistakes in the effort toward building a reputation as an "insecure overachiever" is more than worth your time reading *The Highflier Handbook*. Insecure is not a criticism or insult about your personality. It evokes the feeling Phil West had when he said, "If you are not completely terrified, then you are not appropriately suited to the seriousness of the situation."

Just as Roger Brossy spoke about a meeting participant saying, "Why do we do that?" or the ability to challenge something not "out of belligerence" but out of trying to figure out why we do things as we do, Keith Kratzberg had something similar to say. First, a little about Keith. Keith is Epson America's President and CEO. His responsibilities include overseeing every aspect of Epson America's business strategy. He joined Epson in 1996 and held continually responsible positions until becoming CEO in July of 2016. He holds an MBA from the Anderson School of Management at UCLA.

Keith had this to say:

> *"There's a guy who has been with us for a while. I was aware of him because of his background in engineering. He went to the same business school as I went to, worked for a consulting company for a while. Consultants can judge and frame and analyze and sort any problem. A few things caught my attention. There was a certain model we had about how the business worked. His team put forth a new idea. I told them, maybe a bit too quickly, "You're not right. That's not how it works." He stuck to his guns. He said, "I*

think things have changed." He would not accept me telling him that he was wrong. He scheduled time with me to explain why he thought things worked differently now. And I was convinced. The fact that he was willing to take me on but very respectfully debated the merits, even though he was quite a few levels down below me. I thought that was a very good sign.

Here's another story. It's about sense of humor. It's about a person who has it and is not afraid to use it. He is not outrageously funny. But it is better than "my dad humor." It is a little quicker and cleverer. But once again he is not afraid to use it. When you put out a joke, it can land flat. If you are giving a speech, the risk of opening with a joke is just that ... a risk. Some people have said maybe he needs to be more mature. Maybe the humor was not well placed. I totally disagree. I think that is a comment made by a person who is scared to make a mistake."

After some more discussion, Keith continued:

"I think the tolerance for ambiguity thing, the courage to speak up and the internal drive to move things forward, are so important. The sense of urgency comes from within, not waiting for it to come from the outside.

And there's another guy as I think about this. He has been a highflier for so long. He left us and was gone for several years. I visited him. I reeled him back. He's like the most competitive guy in the world. To his credit, for business. He's great working with people and all that but he wants to win. He thinks, "All this other stuff doesn't matter. Are we winning?" These are shining stars that have different tones to them."

The TNT to file from Keith is messaging and actions that speak to courage, a character trait. Here is just one example of how to take on someone more senior when you are in the beginning of your career that shows courage while remaining responsible to the need to be respectful to the entire team. After all, I want you to be seen and heard as a team player too.

Instead of saying, "I disagree, and I will tell you why," I encourage you to say, "Here's the case I would make and that I think others may make as well. The right step is to move this forward as follows." Once that is said, you should then say, "Having said that, you make a credible argument for your position. I totally get that. Your facts make so much sense." At that point, I encourage you to summarize by saying, "On balance, the upside of the alternative I'm proposing outweighs the data you bring forward."

I want you to be recognized for the work you have done to understand both or even more reasons to support a decision. Not only does saying those things out loud speak to your character, it also speaks to your strategic thinking ability, as I discuss in Chapter 3.

Optimism's Role in Character

An interviewee, Don Robert, Chairman of the London Stock Exchange, contributed a terrific anecdote as well. If you Google Don you'll see biographical material that will set a standard for achievement. Here's just a piece of that. Don Robert is Chairman of London Stock Exchange Group plc, and he has held this position since May 2019. He was Chair of Experian plc, a multinational consumer information company, from 2014 until July 2019. Prior to this he was Group Chief Executive Officer of Experian North America. He had also held senior executive roles at The First American Corporation, Credco, Inc., and served as Chairman of the U.S. Consumer Data Industry Association.

Here's what he had to say about a highflier.

"There was a fellow who is in a key sales position at the London Stock Exchange. He impressed me early. I mean instantly. I still meet with him regularly to stay in touch. I am thinking more about his qualities than anything specific he said. We have had a few meetings now and I cannot tell you the exact phrases or turns of a phrase or words that were used. But he had bankable qualities that I picked up on right away. The sorts of highfliers I am attracted to share these qualities I saw in him. The one most related to character is optimism and enthusiasm. He did say, 'I am nine months or twelve months or fifteen months into the role and I could not be happier that I landed here. The products I have been given to sell are world beating. We can absolutely kick everyone's butt in the industry. It will take a bit of work.' At that point he articulated the plan. It is so common to kick a bunch of people under the bus and do it quickly. People sometimes say, 'I was handed a mess. I am trying to dig us out of that hole.' That is not good. It is not the mark of a highflier. He went on to say, 'You know, we have great raw materials, great markets, and great clients. We will need to make some tough decisions, some changes.'

Now the second thing that impressed me with this guy is he was sitting in the Chairman's office. That can be intimidating. And he was there without notes. He was completely comfortable in his own skin. He could back up every element of his assessment. He did not have a dozen metrics. He had one or two key metrics. 'I think we can take sales per head from seven million to nine million a year. That translates to a billion a year in additional revenue.

We can eliminate an entire sales force because they haven't sold anything in the last six years. I can move that into the Chicago tele center.' He was so completely in command of the facts. He could articulate a credible plan backed up by facts and metrics. So ... comfortable in his own skin and leading with optimism."

You, reader, are renting space in my brain as we look at the TNT growing out of what Don Robert said. We are in a chapter about character, but his description melds into other issues I will cover in this book. Here is what we know a highflier needs to make sure is evident: their optimism. The primary TNT here is to predict a positive outcome if "we do the right things," and avoid a pessimistic outcome if we do not do the right things. There are always two choices.

I am pushing you toward optimism if we move in the right direction. "If we make some tough decisions, some changes we will reach our goals as laid out in the strategy." Avoid, "I am worried that if we maintain the status quo, the future is a minefield." This predicting of positive outcomes is good on its face.

But the more interesting reason for it, with someone like Don Robert who is a classic entrepreneur, is that entrepreneurs are fierce risk takers and, on top of that, are fiercely optimistic that the risk can pay off. If you are in the middle of a message about all the bad things that will happen, the entrepreneur is already thinking about how these things can be overcome.

A Few Words About Words

There are few TNTs for words that are important and filled with meaning. There are a few ideas, however, to keep in mind. Simple

English is thought to have more "meaning" than Latinate English. I am not going to give you a lecture here on linguistics. So many of the old English words are one syllable. I encourage you to give some time to studying this. If I wanted to say something to you hoping it would give you a sense of my feeling for the things that worry you, it would sound more like this: "I want you to know I am here. I want to think that having me near will bring you some peace," and less like this: "It's imperative for you to acknowledge the fact that I am present. I believe that my presence in proximity to you will be a potential blessing."

Can you feel it? Can you feel the power of one syllable words? At the risk of taking some criticism for repeating what I wrote years ago in my book *So Smart But...: How Intelligent People Lose Credibility— and How They Can Get it Back*, here's a line by someone who was known for empathy. Maya Angelou wrote: "You may shoot me with your words, You may cut me with your eyes, You may kill me with your hatefulness, But still, like air, I'll rise."

I am asking you to focus on the writing style. Not only is it one syllable, it also features the figure of speech called epistrophe. That is repeating the first word in three phrases. If you call someone who needs your empathy one day, you could find yourself saying, "You come to mind at times like this. You have a way of making people want to be near you. You give so much to all of us."

I should also say that I do not think I am as good at creating words in a message from scratch as many of my clients. I think of myself as a better editor. The analogy I have always used is this: "We are like a songwriting team. Like Elton John and Bernie Taupin. You, my client, are Bernie. You write the songs. I am like Elton in the sense that I can help with the delivery and comment on the words in the songs; my words may make it better. But you, sir and ma'am, write the words to your presentation."

If you are a person who lives and breathes empathy, kindness, caring, and love, I can help with words that may convey those qualities. Check out Cyrano de Bergerac. If you are not such a person, and there are plenty of them around, my advice will not get you to the finish line. My advice may, however, get you started because, as a behaviorist, I think we start with the action and the feeling will follow.

Chapter 5

Composure Under Pressure

We were all amazed at his ability to keep his cool under the circumstances.

One of my current CEO clients, reaching out to me by email for some advice, said, "Some Gen Z'ers who report to me have terrible eye contact and are intimidated by those of us who refuse to look at our feet when we speak." Her comment about eye contact is a good place to start this chapter.

I have laid out a few TNTs for executive composure and presence in Chapter 2. Composure under pressure is a special niche in the overall presence category, and I cover it in this chapter.

Pressure Can Change Your Normal Style

Looking and sounding composed, especially under pressure, is not entirely a matter of style, but style plays a huge role in it.

When you leave a room after you have expressed your opinion or simply given an update on a project, the words used by others to describe how you did are either, "They *looked* calm and composed" (or didn't) or "They *sounded* calm and composed" (or didn't). Whatever adjective is used to describe you, the opening words are "looked it" or "sounded it." There are so many potential impressions you leave, including prepared, thoughtful, insightful, dependable, energetic, etc.

As you can see in this chapter, the impressions are about composure. People are more likely to say things like that than they are to remember the actual words you used. The earlier comment about eye contact makes that point. There are exceptions to that rule, and I will talk about them in another chapter. There are thoughts so beautifully composed that they will be at the heart of the post-meeting comments. And I will write about that, too. But for now, handling yourself in a manner that results in compliments about your leadership ability cannot be overemphasized.

This is not to say that your message is not as important as the style people saw and heard when you spoke. Your message either provokes the outcome you want, or it does not. It's just that the memories held by the people in that meeting are more likely to come alive through the style you display as you speak to them. For that reason, this chapter is primarily about nonverbal communication.

Keeping It Simple

Here's an example of that. Jeff Immelt, the former CEO of General Electric, sat for a podcast with Matt Abrahams in June 2021. At the time, Immelt had taken a position at the Stanford Graduate School of Business. The title of the podcast was "Leading from the Hot Seat: How to Communicate Under Pressure." Matt asked Immelt for his advice about word choice: "How do you pick specific *words or vocabulary* based on the audience you're speaking to?" (I used italics for *words or vocabulary* to emphasize that Abrahams asked for words!) The question was served up like a fastball down the center of the plate.

Immelt said, "The thing that Jack Welch did better than anybody I've seen before or after, is just his ability to run an organization at scale. So, when he was in front of us communicating to the entire company, it would be words that were simple, themes that were consistent, aspirational but tough-minded. When he was running a meeting, he would be more specific, he would be more pointed, he would be the ranges of highs and lows. The voice which was to the entire community was challenging, but calm. In a meeting it could be excitable. And when he was down to the individual, he was extremely specific in terms of performance and expectations." (Abrahams and Immelt 2021)

Immelt remembered what the outcome of the words would be, not the words themselves. Think about some of those outcomes: consistent themes, aspirational, tough-minded, pointed in ranges of highs and lows. Others included challenging but calm, excitable. I do not know if he remembered the specific words Jack Welch used, but he did not speak to them in this podcast. It is a perfect example of the fact that people remember outcomes you evoke while you speak and not the words themselves.

When you collect your thoughts, for instance, prior to a presentation, you are going to be spending a lot of energy on writing style. You will start putting words to your thoughts and those words are put into sentences with an eye toward syntax, for instance, and that is a style issue. When you think to yourself, "I better not have too many vocalized pauses tomorrow," you are thinking about style. You want to "maintain your composure," so you worry about all those "uhhhs." When people say things like, "It was a word salad," you can tell immediately that the words are not the issue. The issue was the style used to put all those words into a coherent message, and "word salad" means they did not cut through all the chaff.

In that same podcast, Immelt had only this to say about the words: "I was looking at some of the papers of my students last week. And just their ability to communicate in very simple phrases, I still think is something that even sophisticated students still need to learn."

Abrahams concurs and says, "Yeah, so simplicity and concision, I think, are two guiding principles for both writing and speaking for sure."

I have so much to tell you about simplicity, but in this chapter, I am going to give you tips on nonverbal style that shows composure under pressure. Nonverbal is the place to concentrate my TNTs for the topic of composure under pressure. That is because the only tip about word choice is, as Abrahams put it, "simplicity and concision." All of this is by way of explaining why I am focused on a few of the seven qualities of nonverbal communication.

Staying Poised

One of my favorite compliments about a client was, "They were so poised." Immelt spoke to that when describing Jack Welch as "challenging but calm." Here's the definition: If an object or a part of your body is poised, it is completely still but ready to move at any moment. It's a French word. I think of a high-wire walker poised on the wire holding the balance bar. They don't move forward. They don't move backward. They simply remain poised and ready to move. If you are asked a tough question and take your time to compose your thoughts, that is you poised before moving forward.

I must have heard this comment a million times: "I use fillers because I am uncomfortable with silence." Yet the silence is an invitation to show poise. And it is achieved through style. Harvard Business Professor Nancy Koehn spoke to Abraham Lincoln's method of leadership: "One of the things Lincoln cultivated in high-stakes situations was to do nothing in the moment. He wasn't living with nonstop social media. But he was constantly bombarded by people and important issues demanding his attention. In such an environment, his rule was that the higher the stakes, the less likely he was to do anything." That is poise. "Take a deep breath and remain as calm as possible … before responding in order to move forward with an actionable plan." (Miller 2019)

As a teaser, the nonverbal category that accounts for pauses instead of "uhhhs," and "ahhhs" is called vocalics or paralanguage. Stay tuned.

Research on Nonverbal Communication

The "bible" of nonverbal communication, literally called *Nonverbal Communication*, was written by Judee K. Burgoon, Laura K. Guerrero, and Kory Floyd. I studied under Judee Burgoon, as well as her husband Mike, at West Virginia. Judee writes, "Relaxation and composure are communicated nonverbally through a set of behaviors that includes asymmetrical leg and arm positions and less random leg and foot movement (Mehrabian 1969; Mehrabian and Ksionzkey 1972). Facial pleasantness, smiling, eye contact, verbal fluency and close proximity also send messages of calmness, relaxation and composure. (Burgoon et al. 1990) Thus nonverbal behaviors that combine to show openness, expressiveness, lack of nervousness, and positive affect communicate relaxation and poise." (Burgoon, Guerrero, and Floyd 2010)

The nonverbal research categories are Haptics (touch), Kinesics (body movement), Oculesics (eye behavior), Proxemics (how we use space), Vocalics (voice behavior), Chronemics (how we use time), and Objectics (adornment). I am going to focus on a few of them that I believe have the greatest risk and reward relative to composure under pressure.

Haptics: The Role of Touch

Haptics is the nonverbal behavior that accounts for the impact of touch. Three ways that touch correlates to composure under pressure are the number of times you touch your own face, the way your own hands touch as you are talking, and the impact of handshakes.

My first job after finishing the doctoral program was teaching classes of law enforcement officers. They were participating in a graduate program in Public Communication that was underwritten by the Carter administration. They taught me as much as I did them. And one thing they explained was that a person who touched their face while being questioned was often "simply nervous." It could imply lying but just as often nervousness.

In an article by Joe Navarro in *Psychology Today*, he writes, "We touch our faces all day long but not always the same way, nor in the same place. Circumstances dictate where we touch and how we touch." In addition, he adds, "The closer a nerve is to our brain, the faster it sends pacifying or calming signals to the brain when touched. As we touch these nerves by stroking the face, touching the face, or even applying pressure on the face, chemicals are released in the brain which help to calm us." One more: "It is pleasing and soothing to stroke beards and cheeks downward, even around the corners of the mouth … as an attempt to de-stress. How much pressure we apply to that downward stroking depends on circumstances—the greater the stress and anxiety we feel, the greater the pressure we apply." (Navarro 2021)

Can you guess what the TNT is going to be? If you are sitting, rest your hands on the tabletop. If you are standing, hold your hands in front of you as if you were holding a can of soda. Your hands will do the right things and they will not move up to your face.

As to hand wringing, Collins Dictionary defines it as this: "If someone wrings their hands, they hold them together and twist and turn them, usually because they are very worried or upset about something." TNT: I've asked my clients to hold a pen between their hands when standing. That has worked most of the time to show composure.

As to handshaking, an article from the American Psychological Association said, "A new study backs up what the etiquette books have been saying all along, that a firm handshake helps make a good first impression for both males and females. The study ... finds that consistent with the etiquette and business literature, there is a substantial relation between the features that characterize a firm handshake (strength, vigor, duration, eye contact and completeness of grip) and a favorable first impression." One more quote: "... a person's handshake ... is related to some aspects of his or her personality. Those with a firm handshake were more extraverted and open to experience and less neurotic and shy than those with a less firm or limp handshake." (American Psychological Association 2000).

Oculesics: The Role of Eye Contact

Very recently I was asked to work with a client on an upcoming presentation to her board. She was, as they say, "all in" with our meetings. The feedback we both received afterward was "... so much better but still lacked enough eye contact." Eye contact studies are called oculesics research. Eye contact is, without a doubt, the most often cited problem in others' perceptions of us when composure is the topic.

In an article in *Inc.*, Sims Wyeth wrote:

- "When you don't look people in the eye, they are less likely to look at you. And when they stop looking at you, they start thinking about something other than what you're saying, and when that happens, they stop listening."

- "When you look a person in the eye, you communicate confidence and belief in your point of view."

- "When your listeners see your eye scanning their faces, they feel invited to engage with you."

The most useful TNT I have passed on to all my clients is to be sure they have eye contact at the ends of sentences. I have emphasized this behavior because, in English, the words at the ends of sentences carry so much of the meaning. If you looked down to start a sentence like "I have so much faith in everyone on this team," I would want you to look up at them on the words "on this team."

Vocalics: The Qualities Communicated Through Your Voice

Another area of research that has so much to do with composure under pressure is called vocalics or paralanguage. In *Nonverbal Communication*, Judee Burgoon writes, "In the course of centuries of expounding on those voice qualities that were thought to be a part of effective speaker delivery, proponents of the elocutionary movement identified several vocal features (Hyde and Hydes 1886) that a good speaker was expected to master." (Burgoon, Manusov, and Guerrero 2010)

In short, those features are pitch, inflection, loudness, emphasis, tempo, pauses, and voice coloring. Let me give you a prime example of inflection and how it could result in the perception that you have lost composure under pressure. This does not always happen in a pressure setting, like a presentation to executives, but you are vulnerable to it in that setting. This is a very important TNT, so I want to be as clear as possible in explaining it.

There is an interesting voice phenomenon typically called "uptalk." I am about to write a sentence out and I want you to read to yourself out loud just as you see it: "Nothing is quite as important to us as what happens over the next three days."

Now I want you to read it just as you see it again with a small change: "Nothing is quite as important to us as what happens over the next three days."

The only change is the period in the first sentence to a comma in the second. Seminar participants often tell me the sound of the last word in the second version sounds as if the speaker is asking a question. I do not hear it that way. It simply sounds to me as if there is more to come, whereas the first sentence makes a point on its own. It is intended to sound decisive. The comma in the second example is said with pitch going up, and that is why it is referred to as "uptalk." If there are a few sentences, one after the other, done the same way, the sound it makes is described by your listeners as "nagging."

Here is the TNT: As you come to the end of a sentence, slow down on the last few words, and it will always come out right. Using the same sentence as the one earlier, say it out loud this way: "Nothing is quite as important to us as what happens over the...next... three...days." No uptalk. Guaranteed.

Something else to think about that is so interesting to me: English is a language with symbols. They are on your keyboard right now. The symbols were invented to help us think about the right tone when we speak. Here they are: . , ! ? The period is there to tell you to end your thought on a downtone. We can call it downtalk. When you prepare a narrative for a presentation and you read some of it instead of memorizing, think about that! Exclamation points direct you to increase volume. Question marks direct you to increase tone an octave or two on the last word in the sentence.

In *Nonverbal Communication*, the authors write, "Twentieth century researchers added accent and fluency (the presence or absence of filled pauses such as 'um' or 'uh' or repetitions or garbled sounds)." (Burgoon, Manusov, and Guerrero 2010) All of these are part and parcel of how paralanguage contributes so much to perceptions of composure under pressure. The last quality, however—fluency—is the one that has so much to do with composure with or without pressure.

Pausing, Pressure Control, and Exuding Calm

One of my interviews was with Bob Brisco. He was named CEO of WebMD Health Corp and Internet Brands company in September

2018. He has been CEO, President, and Director of Internet Brands since 1999. Before that, Bob was President of Universal Studios Hollywood and City Walk. Bob served as consultant with McKinsey & Co. and the Boston Consulting Group. He was named Entrepreneur of the Year 2012 Greater Los Angeles.

Bob had a couple examples of highfliers. I have a place in this book for them as you will see (like in Chapter 3). But interestingly enough, Bob demonstrated a terrific ability to speak fluently ... that is, with a total absence of fillers. He did it by allowing long and silent pauses before finding just the right word. He was not afraid of losing me while that word came to him. It created a dramatic pause as I waited. It was, just as it is said, "keeping me on the edge of my seat."

Here is an example of something he said in the interview. I will indicate the pauses. You will have to imagine the actual sound of his voice.

> *"I have this habit that my staff would tell me about [pause] which is fine. When something gets very [pause] complicated, which many of our business problems do, I ask a lot of questions. I try to understand what the pieces of the puzzle are. And then I often go [pause] quiet. I typically close my eyes in a meeting and there could be only one person in it [pause] which is awkward I guess for them."*

If you read that back to yourself but say "um" where you see my [pause] you'll know immediately how effective his pauses are.

Now I want you to see how composure came up as a central theme in my talk with Bob. He asked me if it would be appropriate to use himself as an example of becoming a highflier after making the wrong move. After this anecdote, he thought of someone else to describe to me as well. But here is Bob's anecdote about himself.

"I was a first year associate at McKinsey. I'm getting my first serious review. The partner who reviewed me said, 'You project out to have all the attributes of someone who becomes a senior partner, but one thing might get in your way: You are too timid in sharing your hypotheses early in a process.' He elaborated. He said, 'There was a moment at the beginning of the engagement where everyone on the senior team was called away. You were left on your own with a whiteboard in the corner. We came back and you had written out a series of hypotheses that we would need to test over the next couple of months that would lead to a favorable and logical conclusion to the project. We were blown away. But we thought, had we not left the room, would we ever have known whether you were any good or not? Because you just sort of sat there and let us do it.' I remember thinking that you have to act like the job one or two steps ahead of the job you have. You have to visualize yourself in that job fully, not arrogantly but in a calm, confident manner, in order for others to perceive that you are actually capable of doing that job."

Bob says, "…in a calm and confident manner." We were not in the room to hear and see what it would have looked like if Bob had expressed his ideas before the senior people left the room. Had we been, based on listening to Bob now, that calmness would have been shown through the slower, pause-filled sentences he uses when he speaks now. I have no doubt that you are filled with great ideas, too. But use Bob's example, demonstrated through paralanguage, to get your ideas heard.

Here's another way to think about this and it's a terrific TNT: Think of all these moments as teaching moments. Think of yourself as a teacher and the others in the room as your students. Ask yourself what it takes in your teaching skills to get your students in a position to take notes, so to speak, and react to your "lesson" as material that is thought provoking. The "teacher" in you is expected to show composure and your "students" in that meeting are evaluating it as you speak.

Composure Measured by Your Manner of Listening

From the start, I wanted to make sure *The Highflier Handbook* had a generous number of anecdotes from senior women about highflying women they have watched grow. I have been fortunate to know many of them or to be introduced to them by others. One of them is Alison Davis. Alison is the Chair and Managing Partner of Blockchain Coinvestors. She has significant experience as a corporate executive, board member, and successful author on technology and innovation. She was named among the "Most Influential Women in Business" by the San Francisco Business Times. She has a BA Honors and a Master's in Economics from Cambridge University as well as an MBA from the Graduate School of Business at Stanford and from Harvard.

Here is what she told me about composure under pressure:

> *"It is not so much one person but so many young people early in their career. There are nine or ten people out of hundreds who are really engaged with good EQ and confidence. If they are in a meeting and they are not thinking, 'I'm so junior and why am I here?' but instead show up very curious and confident and articulate and composed, you love to see them. They ask good questions, contribute a point of view, and do it early in a way that is not obnoxious. You love to see them because it is not that common. With a lot of people their head gets in the way or*

they are not fully in it. They seem not so interested in what they are doing that they cannot help themselves. You love to see someone who has poise, confidence, is articulate and engaged and trying to participate."

The manner and style you show as a listener implies you are "all in" and not distracted in focus. The speaker sees that as a sign of your composure through the conversation. There is more to come, but I want to take a moment for a huge TNT here. The description of people who show up curious, who have good questions and are "fully in it," is shown primarily through listening behavior. I have compared talented speaking to good teaching. Now I want to compare talented listening to being a good student. To be a highflier, you have to sit in a meeting, real or virtual, and behave in a way that your "teachers" will recognize immediately as engaged students. It is a test of your ability to react in an engaging way. Sometimes it's with words like "That makes sense" or "Here's an alternative take on that." Often it includes a facial expression that appears totally alert.

Alison began describing one particular young woman at McKinsey where she worked for a time.

"I was in charge of a project where there was a new analyst on the team. We were working for a manufacturing company in the Midwest. She did not have expertise in manufacturing, and it was a logistic project. She showed up and began asking good questions. She was willing to say, 'Can you unravel that a bit for me?' or 'What did you mean by that?' She was clearly not daunted by the fact that she was new. She is 21 years old, looked people right in the eye, people in their 40s who are the kind of clients we're dealing with and we have questions we are trying to pursue. She was right in there connecting with them in a friendly way.

It came across as 'you can trust me as I try to understand.' Many young people could do that, but I think their mind gets in the way of being fearful or afraid to bring their best selves to the situation. There is pressure and she kept her cool and composed persona intact. She was friendly and laughed and made a personal comment. She connected with the client. By the end of the meeting, they liked her. There was human warmth there."

It is TNT time. A piece of this young woman's demeanor described as composed was related to her being so interested in the people she was serving. I have started most introductory calls with a new client, who may be somewhat perplexed by the situation they find themselves in, by first asking about their personal, not academic, background or the feedback they've had. It's like me to ask where they were born and what their hobbies are and where they went to school. I have so often joked with them about how hard it will be to work with me if they went to a school that beat West Virginia in football. At the top of the list is Pittsburgh. (OK. Now you know where my insecurity comes from when it comes to being an insecure overachiever. It is losing to Pitt!)

At the conclusion of our interview, Alison added this:

"Performance is only 20 percent of it. Your image is your brand. What do people think of you and say about you? Do people say, 'Wow, that person's brand is all about the company. They lean in and are easy to work with.' And how many people know you? Do you sit in your cubical and work really hard? Or are you out there and have lots of connectivity in the company and in the industry? It is performance times image times exposure. That really rings a bell for me. They are smart but you do not need to be that smart. Your performance ... just ... needs ... to ... be ... good."

You can see by those pauses how much emphasis she put on the concluding thought. And do not forget my example of slowing down the words at the end of a sentence. No uptalk from Alison.

Taking a Challenge and Running with It

Another interview I am going to reveal for you was with Dan Kirby. He is the CEO of Orca Bio. I wanted you to see this one because he described a very pressurized situation for a highflier. Dan is responsible for their cell therapy platform including Orca T, their lead cell therapy asset. He leads Orca's efforts in market engagement and the reimbursement landscape. He has been the Chief Commercial Officer at Ormeros Corporation and prior to that was VP of US Commercial Cell and Gene Therapy at Celgene. Celgene grew out of the Juno Therapeutics acquisition. Prior to Juno, Dan was the Head of Marketing for Medivation as well as spending 14 years at Amgen.

Dan shared this anecdote:

> *"At Amgen they had rotations of people coming out of blue-chip MBA programs. They did internships, 18 months in the field and 18 months on a marketing team. I had been awarded one of these. The person had an MD from Drexel and their MBA from Wharton. Very bright guy. The training people called me. They said he had his feet on the table during training. Because he was smarter than everybody else, the training people took it all in stride. Someone did talk to him about that. Then he joined my team. I put this person in an extremely stressful situation. I told them, you are not going to have one territory or shadow off someone else's work. Usually, you would put them in a territory, split the workload and then whether they worked or not that person in the territory would do the work anyway. Therefore, they would just be away, they check the box.*

I gave him 50 targets in the New York metro area. I gave him messages to give those doctors and I wanted to see six messages done in two months to every ... single ... one ... of those doctors. You could call them six times. Whatever you do in that call, you need to see those things. And we are going to track your performance and what you do. We will see how you perform against the group. He hated it. He didn't have a territory to backdraft off of so we had to pick his doctors. He was plotted every month against what he was doing and not against one rep but against five reps. He embraced the challenge. He came up with his own analytics and showed me different reports using his analytical skill sets to show me exactly how the messages were sticking and what was happening. He was outperforming the nation. He did not flinch. He joked around with the team and became one of them ... He embraced the challenge in front of him. I challenged him, he stepped up to it. He showed us a new path in how to do things. That is a great example of giving someone a challenge, putting them under a tremendous amount of pressure, and seeing how well they responded. He has a huge career now."

This anecdote should remind you of what Phil West of Steptoe said in Chapter 4. In essence, a healthy dose of paranoia to make sure you are on top of things impresses everyone around you in times of stress. The TNT about this story is to do more than you are asked and create analytics that help achieve the strategy. The focus required to exceed expectations, and that maybe include the detail work involved in creating analytics, is a continual demonstration of your ability to remain composed and controlled.

Control When the Unexpected Occurs

Finally I want you to hear the anecdote related by Andy McCullough. I worked with him at Kaiser Permanente for a number of years. Andy was president of the Kaiser Foundation Hospitals and Health Plan for the Northwest beginning in 2006. It was ranked among the highest performing health systems in the United States. He was a recipient of the Regent's Award from the American College of Healthcare Executives. He also received the Gaylord W. Anderson MD Leadership Award from the University of Minnesota's School of Public Health. He was among those named as a Top 10 Executive of the Year as a result of leading Kaiser's membership growth.

Here's what Andy had to say:

"There was a vacancy on the senior leadership team. I was tired of the standard interview process. There are so many ways people can, well, I would not say manipulate ... well, let's just say it is not always precise given the important decisions that must be made. The way we used to test candidates, once we decided on two people, was to give them an actual problem we as a senior team were grappling with. We brought the two finalists in and said, 'We want you to give a presentation and facilitate a discussion around this problem we are dealing with.' We did not interrupt them as they led the discussion on the issue and wanted to see if they could bring the group to a higher level of understanding and consensus.

We asked them what they needed in the way of visual aids. We had a projector so they could plug their computer in and share slides. The first time we did this, the projector bulb went out. The candidate could not use it. We felt like we had screwed up. It turned out to be an amazing insight into how to deal with adversity on your feet. The person who got the job did not miss a beat. They said, 'No problem. I have hardcopy backups.' The ability to deal with adversity, keep your composure, adapt to a change in circumstances, was a value we looked for. We might not have found it without this situation. We incorporated it for every interview after that."

The ability to handle a presentation, often called a "set piece," had better be in the wheelhouse of every consultant who describes themselves as communication experts. There have been a myriad of books on this topic ever since Dale Carnegie started programs on *How to Win Friends and Influence People.*

I want to leave you with one TNT, otherwise this chapter on Composure Under Pressure will start to read like another book on public speaking. If you look at Chapter 3, I described a framework for a presentation: TAR, which stands for Title, Agenda, and Result. I am going to tack an "S" at the beginning of that framework and we will call it STAR. The "S" stands for Story or Setting Context. At the very beginning, after what I always call the pleasantries—"Good morning. Great to be here," etc.—open with an anecdote. It will calm you down as you strive to stay composed as well as serve as an attention grabber for everyone listening. Anecdotes are very much like children's stories that start with "Once upon a time." But for adults, the opening words should be something like, "About a month ago..."

Here's an example: "About a month ago I was working with a team of people preparing for a product launch. We were hard at work figuring out exactly when and where to introduce it to the media. I met with the CEO one morning at breakfast. She asked me how enthusiastic we were as we planned. I said, 'I have never been with people more prepared and ready to jump into this as this group is.'"

Then I want you to say, "That feeling is at the heart of what I want to talk about today."

As a highflier you will always attract attention from the people who come to know you. It will be for the way you act and speak as you work, as well as from your leisure time manner. So many of my interviewees cited listening as a major source of that attention. I'll tackle listening in Chapter 6.

Listening

I was impressed by how much extreme effort went into listening.

Over the years, whenever clients talk to me about Stephen R. Covey and his book *The 7 Habits of Highly Effective People,* they first use the phrase "listen for understanding." Actually, Habit 5 is entitled "Seek First to Understand, Then to Be Understood." Covey wrote that this habit

> *"involves a very deep shift in paradigm. We typically seek first to be understood. Most people do not listen with the intent to understand; they listen with the intent to reply. They're either speaking or preparing to speak. They're filtering everything through their own paradigms, reading their autobiography into other people's lives."*
>
> *—(Covey 1989)*

So how do you live up to this ideal? One answer to that question came up in Chapter 5. Alison Davis described a highflier having this quality. It is worth repeating here:

> *"It is not so much one person but so many young people early in their career. There are nine or ten people out of hundreds who are really engaged with good EQ and confidence.*

If they are in a meeting, and they are not thinking, 'I'm so junior and why am I here?' but instead show up very curious and confident and articulate and composed, you love to see them. They ask good questions, contribute a point of view, and do it early in a way that is not obnoxious. You love to see them because it is not that common. With a lot of people their head gets in the way or they are not fully in it. You love to see someone who has poise, confidence, is articulate and engaged and trying to participate."

It All Began with Carl Rogers

Now, let me take you back to where all the emphasis on listening skills began, when all the seminars on listening skills took root. It's embodied in the work of psychologist Carl Rogers. He is responsible for the term "active listening," and that phrase will be on the lips of anyone who does listening skills seminars. In the book *Communicating in Business Today*, the authors write, in commenting about active listening:

"Active listening does not necessarily mean long sessions spent listening to grievances, personal or otherwise. It is simply a way of approaching those problems which arise out of the usual day-to-day events of any job.

To be effective, active listening must be firmly grounded in the basic attitudes of the user. We cannot employ it as a technique if our fundamental attitudes are in conflict with its basic concepts. If we try, our behavior will be empty and sterile, and our associates will be quick to recognize this. Until we can demonstrate a spirit which genuinely respects the potential worth of the individual, which considers his sights and trusts his capacity for self-direction, we cannot begin to be effective listeners.

Active listening is an important way to bring about changes in people. Despite the popular notion that listening is a passive approach, clinical and research evidence clearly shows that sensitive listening is a most effective agent for individual personality change and group development. Listening brings about changes in people's attitudes toward themselves and others; it also brings about changes in their basic values and personal philosophy. People who have been listened to in this new and special way become more emotionally mature, more open to their experiences, less defensive, more democratic, and less authoritarian."

—(Rogers and Farson 1987)

My practice is built on the notion of technique. I am not being responsible to you if I do not give you technique through tips, as you have seen. Rogers warns you that your use of his techniques must not be artificial, or you will be discovered, so to speak. I am going to describe some Rogerian technique here and then write about how highfliers would use them and not be called out as "faking it." I am personally invested in this "faking it" or lack of "authenticity" issue as it came up not long ago in a speech I gave in the Silicon Valley.

I must write this first: All of us are a combination of nature and nurture. The nature part is at the heart of "relax and be yourself." It is like saying, "Rely on your nature." Nurture is a result of all we've been taught since birth. And it's been a legitimate part of the whole ever since. If we are, in fact, known for humility, we were either born with it or followed the modeling of adults or both—maybe parents or guardians or role models or Sunday School.

I have been privileged to offer advice. My career is built on that. There are examples of advice that very few clients would reject out of hand. For instance, encouraging someone to speak louder at a meeting to be heard or to exude a higher level of energy has not resulted, so far, in making my client feel his or her "true self" is at risk. But I have experienced pushback on the advice to nod your head more often when you are listening if it is not natural.

Many listening skill suggestions are like that. Rogers might teach listeners to say things like, "Let me repeat what you've said to make sure I'm tracking you correctly." Both Carl Rogers and Allen Weiner are betting that the risk of deploying a behavioral tip you are not naturally inclined to do is worth the outcome—the outcome that you would be described as a wonderful listener. If someone felt that you were only saying that because you were taught to say it and that it was not the "real you," it is like discouraging someone's effort to be nurturing. But at the heart of it, that is why all of us do this work. Please ... reread this whenever you have doubts about your true and authentic self.

Now, continuing with the suggestions around technique, Rogers writes,

> *"Active listening aims to bring about changes in people. To achieve this end, it relies upon definite techniques—things to do and things to avoid doing... .*
>
> *The active-listening approach ... does not present a threat to the individual's self-picture. He does not have to defend it. He is able to explore it, see it for what it is, and make his own decision about how realistic it is. And he is then in a position to change... .*
>
> *Just what does active listening entail, then? Basically, it requires that we get inside the speaker, that we grasp, from his point of view, just what it is that he is communicating to us. More than that, we must convey to the speaker that we*

are seeing things from his point of view. To listen actively,
then, means that there are several things we must do."
—*(Rogers and Farson 1987)*

In Chapter 3, I talked about your ability to articulate an opinion contra to your own, after expressing your own, and helping your listener understand *how well you have been listening to them.* I wrote about it as a part of strategic thinking because it also has the benefit of demonstrating that quality, too. It's called a two-sided message: "Educated people are usually capable of thinking of at least a few opposing arguments for themselves and might be suspicious of the motives of a speaker who does not consider these same arguments." (Burgoon and Ruffner 1977)

Put that together with what Covey wrote and I quoted earlier in this chapter: "Seek first to understand … involves a very deep shift in paradigm. We typically seek first to be understood. Most people do not listen with the intent to understand; they listen with the intent to reply." A highflier will be seen and heard as letting the other people in the room know they have heard and actually honor the "other side."

Here comes the TNT courtesy of both Covey and Rogers: When there are people in the room who have a different opinion than yours, they want to know you have heard them and understand them. In that setting, here is my recommendation. You will say something like, "I think _____. I say that because of _____ and _____. Here's some data that supports that. [Talk about your approach.] Now having said that, I hear what you are saying. You have clear concerns about that. Your logic is based on _____ and ____ if I understand you as you intended. I get that. It's just that on balance, I think the upside, the benefits of my approach, outweighs the upside of your approach."

Respecting Others' Opinions Shows Humility

One of the executives I spoke with was Chuck Davidson. Chuck is a Venture Partner at Quantum and a member of QEP's Investment Committee. Prior to joining Quantum, Chuck served as CEO of Noble Energy from 2000 to 2014 and as its Chairman until his retirement in May 2015. Before joining Noble Energy, Chuck was Chairman, President, and Chief Executive Officer of Vastar Resources, Inc. Prior to Vastar, he served in executive assignments at ARCO. Chuck holds a BS in chemical engineering from Purdue University and an MBA from the University of Texas at Dallas.

Here's what Chuck had to say about a highflier that stood out to him:

> *"I was asked to become the engineering manager in East Texas. I was totally unqualified to do that job. But I was asked to do it and I did it. I had a young engineer from A&M. He was just incredible. And was going up like a sky-rocket. He was a leader on that team, even though he was only a few years out of school. But he had the poise, the confidence, he had the humility, he had the ability to respect the opinions of others. I judge a lot of people based on their ability to listen. Are they listening or are they just talking? And the ones who usually rise to the top, in my view, are those who listen. That is really important."*

Chuck continued:

> *"I'm not done. There's someone else. He was at Vastar. ARCO took Vastar public in 1994. I had an engineer there who was doing planning for us. First of all, he was a really nice person. But again, he was thoughtful. It was not like*

*he had just his own opinion. He was somebody who lis-
tened to and appreciated other opinions. I knew this was
an incredible individual who would really go far."*

Chuck remembered yet another individual and had this to say:

*"Someone recently referred to me as his mentor. That is quite
an honor for me ... for any of us. He had the same characteristics I have been talking about with you. He sought
input, sought the advice of others, listened to them and
incorporated them into his thinking. He became a fantastic
leader, not only of his own company but of our industry."*

The TNT that matters most in Chuck's interview is the power of
asking for advice. I encourage you to make your colleagues' opinions and suggestions seem critical to your own view of things. Treat
them as if they were external consultants who have earned your
respect. For example:

- "How did you come to that conclusion?"
- "Who should I go to for a clearer description?"
- "Where would be the best place to test it out?"

Taking the Temperature of the Room

I wanted to hear from attorneys and their "discovery" of highfliers
because their profession is so dependent on communication skill.
Kevin Muck and Susan Muck sat for a combined interview. They
both had insights about highfliers in regards to listening. For 36 years
Kevin has represented clients in a wide range of industries, including
life sciences, software, data storage and security, financial services,

and many others. He has represented Fortune 100 companies as well as high-profile private companies. He joined Wilmer Hale in San Francisco in 2020 after 15 years at another Bay Area law firm where he co-founded the securities litigation practice.

Susan Muck has practiced law in the Bay Area for more than three decades. She has been a trusted advisor to many of the region's most innovative companies. In addition, she is a founding member of Women in Securities, a network for women securities litigators, and is an active member of the Women's White Collar Defense Association. She is currently a partner with Wilmer Hale.

Kevin's sense of the benefits of great listening includes the ability to calm people down and give comfort to his clients. He said of one highflier, "The demeanor was perfect. He was very calming and that, as well as being organized, gave comfort to his clients. Through his listening, he was able to help them focus on what they could control."

One of the qualities Susan referenced with the highflier she spoke to me about was the ability to "take the measure of the room with a board they did not know previously. Within a few minutes they began to understand the temperature of most of the board members, who were 15 different people both male and female. They were able to kind of assess which of the individuals were the most dominant and which were not. They figured out who they needed to direct most of the message to. He could assess which were the most nuanced thinkers and not to offend anyone … that is taking the measure of the room so that when it was time to speak, everyone felt included."

Think about the value your listening, active or otherwise, brings when other people think of you. People working with you can potentially describe you with compliments about your humility, your ability to take the measure of the room, your calming influence, your ability to incorporate the views of others, and your respect for the people you work with. If ever there was a gigantic case for the behavior to result in such wonderful benefits, it is in this case ... the case for showing how well you listen.

I wrote earlier that clients are often resistant to behavioral suggestions like nodding your head a bit while you are listening. I am not surprised that there are behaviors my clients feel odd trying out if it is something unnatural. But look at the potential benefit. Here is what Carl Rogers writes that makes it all worthwhile.

> *"By consistently listening to a speaker, you are convey-ing the idea that: 'I'm interested in you as a person, and I think that what you feel is important. I respect your thoughts, and even if I don't agree with them, I know that they are valid for you. I feel sure that you have a contri-bution to make. I'm not trying to change you or evaluate you. I just want to understand you. I think you're worth listening to, and I want you to know that I'm the kind of person you can talk to.'"*
> —*(Rogers and Farson 1987)*

To be fair to Carl Rogers and to you, I need to give you examples of the behaviors or wording that it is suggested you use to be a good active listener. TNTs are coming.

- Look the talker in the eye if you are both in the same room or on a virtual call. I have already reminded you to nod. If you are on a conference call, use your voice to indicate you are still present. Say things like "got it," "right," even "uh huh." Whatever you utter, it will be better than total silence.

- Taking notes as the talker proceeds is exceptionally rare for them and signals heightened attention from you.

- Echo back, to some extent, what you think you are hearing. For instance, if the speaker says, "We are up against it time wise," your response could be, "I can hear the stress as you speak."

- Ask questions of the talker because it shows something they said was thought-provoking and you want to hear more. For instance, if the speaker says, "I left the meeting thinking we were aligned," you could ask, "What exactly did you hear that gave you that impression?"

- In the attempt to help solve a problem, you could say "How can we make this whole effort more manageable?" This is a recommendation from principal Mandy Land (The Holdsworth Center 2020). Her advice is even more sensible when it is a conference call and people cannot see you but only hear you.

When it comes to listening, I am more cautious about giving you the words to use than I am the nonverbal cues like nodding and eye contact or sitting up and looking interested or taking notes, etc. As you can see, however, I have gone out on a limb, so to speak, to do just that. I am cautious because I like to hear the words my clients would use since they will come to them more naturally than practicing my version. I have often said, "You, my client, and I are like a songwriting team. You are the lyricist. I am more comfortable doing the arrangement." Many times, they have asked me for potential wording of any message and I have done my best. But overall, looking at these examples, I trust you to use the words that spring up naturally and put them in the form, the arrangement you see here.

Facial Expression, Intended or Not, Conveys Your Attitude

Amy Gallo wrote a piece for the Harvard Business Review titled "What Is Active Listening?" At one point she writes, "Active listening is when you not only hear what someone is saying, but also attune to their thoughts and feelings. It turns a conversation into an active, non-competitive, two-way interaction." (Gallo 2024)

She cites Robin Abrahams and Boris Groysberg from Harvard Business School as describing active listening as having three aspects: cognitive, emotional, and behavioral.

> *"Cognitive: Paying attention to all the information, both explicit and implicit, that you are receiving from the other person, comprehending, and integrating that information.*
>
> *Emotional: Staying calm and compassionate during the conversation, including managing any emotional reactions (annoyance, boredom) you might experience.*
>
> *Behavioral: Conveying interest and comprehension verbally and nonverbally."*

Abrahams and Groysberg write in an article titled "How to Become a Better Listener":

> *"Getting good at active listening is a lifetime endeavor. However, even minor improvements can make a big difference in your listening effectiveness."*
>
> *—(Abrahams and Groysberg 2021)*

Finally, for our purposes here, Abrahams and Groysberg write, "Eye contact, attentive posture, nodding and other nonverbal cues are important, but it's hard to pay attention to someone's words when you're busy reminding yourself to make regular eye contact." Gallo advises, "At some point in the conversation, you'll likely need to share your perspective but, for now, take in what they have to say. It's far better to ask questions—it makes the other person feel listened to and increases your comprehension."

One of the TNTs I need to explain is the way that question-asking magnifies your ability to listen. In other words, you are bringing out information from others that gives you that more of a chance to show how well you listen. After hearing someone speak, you have at least four options as a response. Two of them are excellent for helping a person decide what they want to say.

The first one is questions that give a speaker a chance to say "yes" or "no" or "I don't know." Even though yes or no questions have been unfairly labeled as closed ended, they rarely result in just a yes or no. The reason responders have much more to say than yes or no is those questions help a responder clarify their own thinking and they feel more confident in expressing themselves. And that allows you to show how well you listen. If you, in a meeting, asked a colleague, "Do you feel pretty confident about the choice we have made?" you are not going to hear a simple yes or no. The responder is going to tell you why they feel as they do. You are making it easier for them to speak and that will make it easier for you to listen. It is quite the opposite of closed ended. It is typically inviting "openness."

The same is true of questions where you offer a speaker a choice of answers. If you asked, "When you think about the choice we have made, are you 100 percent committed to it or are you wavering until you hear more?" the speaker can relax a bit and take a moment to choose the way they feel. Once again, you have given them a calming moment and that partly explains what Kevin Muck said earlier about a highflier's ability to calm the room.

If you ask the traditional open-ended question so often endorsed by just about every writer on communication skills, you may be asking for answers that are difficult to process. And asking someone in a meeting a question starting with "Why…" is going to make them feel defensive. Defensiveness is typically shown with overly detailed answers. So there are two consequences: a lot of extraneous detail that is hard to listen to and creating defensiveness in someone unintentionally.

In the samples shown earlier with yes/no questions and questions offering choices, one of the examples was, "Do you feel comfortable with the choice we made?" If instead you asked the open-ended question "Why do you feel comfortable with the choice we have made?" you are inviting them to worry about the quality of the logic revealed in their answer. If there are few people in the room, that worry is magnified. Now I am not suggesting that you should always be concerned with how worried someone is because of your questions. But that worry will create a situation that makes it harder for you to be a good listener. It is not a calming moment. Chances are, you will hear why they feel as they do as the conversation continues.

Encouraging the Speaker to Say More

There is an interesting online resource called the Social Science Research Modules Project. The project directors are Netta Avineri, Lisa Gates, Matt Lawrence, and Phil Murphy. One of the modules in the project is on active listening. Adding to the list of benefits, they cite communicating empathy and building trust. They offer three behavioral suggestions including (1) expressing interest, (2) paraphrasing to make sure you understand while refraining from judgment, and (3) asking questions to encourage the speaker to elaborate.

I have reminded you in the previous section about some of the issues with question asking. I have not, however, given you a TNT about paraphrasing. In the Project, the authors write that some questions, as we now know, can result in elaborate answers. For instance, "If you asked, 'How has the transition to a remote classroom affected learning?' it will elicit a lengthy response." They write, "You can reflect the participant's response back by saying, 'what I am hearing you say is you've noticed an improvement in your students' technological skills.'"

The TNT here is that the paraphrase is short. I often recommend a response about the same length as the statement that elicited it.

Another TNT: I suggest you use the words "What I am hearing you say is..." sparingly. I have heard feedback about clients, as we start an engagement, that someone using that phrase too often results in a perception that they "have been to a listening skills class." You could just as easily say, "So you've seen an improvement..." (or whatever you happen to be paraphrasing).

A Skilled Talker Can Make Listening a Pleasure

Michael Burgoon and Michael Ruffner write in their book *Human Communication* about the physical and psychological factors that influence good listening. Of course, your ability to hear, without belaboring the point, will make it hard to hear the spoken word. Your ability to understand a speaker's words cannot be ignored. If the message is too complex or your vocabulary is limited, you are going to look confused. If the speaker has a strong and unfamiliar accent, you will find yourself struggling to understand the message, both each word and the overall logic.

We also differ in our relative ability to remember what someone has said despite how we try to concentrate as they are talking. Some researchers predicted that if listeners anticipated what they were about to hear, their comprehension increased. (Brown 1959)

I want to conclude this chapter with an alternative way to look at the entire process of talking and listening skills. Who has the responsibility for enhanced listening? Is it listeners themselves who need to be reminded of how to practice their listening behavior, as we have done in this chapter, or is it the speaker who needs to be reminded of how to speak in a compelling and provocative way to ensure a listener's interest?

As Burgoon and Ruffner wrote, "Everyone enjoys listening to a clever and entertaining speaker discussing an interesting topic, but what happens when the speaker is humorless, the topic boring, and the vocabulary difficult? In such a situation, the inexperienced listener is likely to turn off all listening powers and begin daydreaming or napping" (Burgoon and Ruffner 1977). If you are lucky, the talker in your next conversation will make it easy for you to be the listener everyone wants you to be. If not … review this chapter.

Chapter 7

Personality

Some people just have it.

Whenever the topic of audience analysis comes up, the common suggestion is to tailor your message to the audience. But audiences are made up of people with unique personalities.

Michael Burgoon and Michael Ruffner wrote in their book *Human Communication*, "It is beneficial to view receivers as individuals possessing a unique personality that will affect their response to a message. For example, outgoingness, shyness, hostility, or anxiety are characteristics of one's personality that remain fairly stable from situation to situation." (Burgoon and Ruffner 1977)

The authors wrote this anticipating that academic readers will want to read theory about personality in order to plan persuasive messages. I included this to make it clear that my purpose in this chapter is less about planning for a presentation and more about the word "personality" as it is used to describe people.

I was reading a biography of Barbara Walters earlier this year. She complained about various people she talked to as "lacking that sparkle." The academic definitions of "personality" cover a vast array of types. But the way the word is often used by people assessing our personality is typically with the shorthand description of "has it" or "doesn't have it." It is in that spirit that I show you, in this chapter, how the word *personality* has been a part of social science research for many years and how you can learn tips for being a highflier based on that.

What Drives Your Behavior?

Lee Ross and Richard Nisbitt wrote a groundbreaking book about personality called *The Person and the Situation*. Malcolm Gladwell is quoted on the cover saying, "This book has been a constant companion over the past 10 years." In essence Ross and Nisbitt describe the debate about whether our personality or the situation we are a part of is more influential in determining our behavior. In other words, do you "sparkle" because that is who you are, or do you sparkle because the situation brought it out in you? Some writers in psychology believe that our personality is baked in, so to speak, and is consistent across situations. Others say that our personality is not consistent enough from setting to setting.

While the academic controversy may be worth your effort to study, one tip I am going to give you now is to be wary of people pigeonholing you as having one predominant personality. In other words, I do not want someone to describe you as an extrovert, or introvert for that matter, as if you will always show that in your daily comings and goings. I want you to be described as having at least a two-dimensional personality. The description would be something like, "When you meet and work with them, you will find them to be exceptionally nice and easy to work with. But make no mistake, they are also, depending on the situation, capable of showing genuine disappointment if people make a commitment and do not adhere to the deadlines."

I want people, particularly the people who choose you to be a part of a team, to know that you are versatile, that you are not just "of a type." Suppose you had the desire to move from one group to another in the same organization. If a phone call was made from the team lead in the new group to the team lead in your present group, the opening statement is going to be "Tell me about them." The response to that is going to start with a statement about "personality."

Suppose it was something like, "Incredibly smart but somewhat introverted. I've had to work with them to speak up at meetings, but it's been a slog." You absolutely would not want that. The best answer would be, "You may find them to be somewhat quiet in some meetings but in others they are very outspoken. It just depends on the topic." That would be sublime! And that is why this chapter is so vital.

So how do you come across as multidimensional? Some research shows that your communication style can affect perceptions of your personality. Gretchen Macht and David Nembhard wrote, "In this study, we consider communication (a key feature of teamwork) as a potentially mediating factor between each aspect of human personality ... and team performance... .Results indicate that at least one team measure of extraversion, agreeableness, neuroticism, and openness is moderated by communication in influencing team performance." (Macht and Nembhard 2015) For example, talking faster vs. slower, talking louder vs. softer, and focusing on details vs. the bigger picture can change the way your personality is perceived.

There are theories and theorists, plenty of them, that argue for personality being more consistent over situations. But my interest in all of this is simply to say that people form opinions of our personality and do not concern themselves with how we got it.

My mentor Jim McCroskey and co-author Jason Teven wrote a piece for *Communication Monographs* that opened with this: "A central aspect of the study of persuasion and social influence from classical times to the present has been the image of the source in the minds of receivers. Aristotle referred to this image as the source's *ethos* and suggested that it was the source's most potent means of persuasion (Cooper 1932). The Yale Group (Hovland, Janis, and

Kelley 1953) echoed Aristotle's view in arguing that *source cred-ibility*, their term for the source's image, was a central aspect in the persuasive effectiveness of any communicator" (McCroskey and Teven 1999). You can immediately sense that when a low or highflier begins to be assessed by others, their personality takes center stage.

There is an excellent and concise summary of the "Big Five" personality dispositions that is extremely thought provoking. Those five are

- Neuroticism

- Extraversion

- Openness to experience

- Agreeableness

- Conscientiousness

Mark Knapp and John Daly write that scholars believe these five incorporate all personality constructs. I encourage you to look fur-ther into these as you become curious about personality and the compliment that you have "IT."

Helping to Develop People

When the results of the research on credibility, as I described in Chapter 1, were initially released, there were five dominant factors: Competence, Composure, Character, Sociability, and High Energy (or Extroversion). Subsequently researchers began looking more deeply into a potential sixth factor. They called it Goodwill. Goodwill is the modern term for ethos that Aristotle introduced to us. Today we might call it collaboration or cooperation. We could call it kindness or bigheartedness.

If and when the opportunity presents itself, I encourage you to be a part of any mentoring program your organization offers. Make it a priority. If someone asks you for advice, give it as wholeheartedly as you can. Avoid phrases like, "It's just something you have to be born with." Even goodwill can result in comments like, "They just have the 'it' factor."

Enthusiasm and Passion

One of my clients over the years has been Marilyn Vetter. She is a dynamo (hence a perfect contributor to this chapter) and had plenty to say about personality. She is an example of "it takes one to know one." First, some information about her: Marilyn is the CEO of Pheasants Forever and Quail Forever, the nation's leading organization committed to conserving upland birds and wildlife through habitat improvement. Marilyn leads a 600-person team. Her leadership extended across the biopharmaceutical sector to the NGO arena. She has expertise in government relations, strategic planning, corporate affairs, and risk oversight. She has lived a lifetime of volunteering with organizations that speak to her passion in life sciences, professional development, civic organizations, and environmental conservation.

Here's what Marilyn had to share:

> *"Let's talk about sincerity. You mentioned that one of your interviewees used the term 'sparkle.' I don't know if it's the word I would use. But it's the characterization of someone who can stimulate inspiration in the people around them by their presence, and by their enthusiasm and their passion. They elicit in others what they hope to elicit in themselves through that very sincere transference of energy and optimism.*

There's a young lady on my team who works in a very challenging state with a very challenging audience. She's 26 or 27. And her audiences, I would say, 75 to 85 percent are older men. I've been involved with Pheasants Forever for 42 years. And we have had people rotate through this job a lot in the last six years. Because they're a tough audience. They have an idea of how things should work. And they've been very helpful and challenging for us to work with. I went to their state meeting this year. And it was fascinating to see how, since she has that same optimism and that same ability to transfer that optimism and a hope for the future to others, she helped them get past their indignation about the way things are compared to how they think they should be. And without any kind of urging on my part, at least a half dozen of those gentlemen came up to me and said, 'I am so thrilled that [she] is on this team, she makes me feel differently about the future than I used to feel.'

I think there's a personality quality, talking about entrepreneurs, and that is a bit of fearlessness. And that for someone like me, at least who I think I am, I tend to have a natural pause. I'm more likely to examine things first. There's a fearlessness with entrepreneurs. They think, 'If I don't get it right, I'll just do something else.' They don't. They don't let that fear stop them. And that's what I think she saw in this audience. She said to herself, it seems to me, 'All I can do is try and I will do what I think might work. And if that doesn't work, we'll just keep trying other things.' And they loved that. I don't think she had to pander to them to do it. But I think she was willing to accept failure, if that's what it was. Because from that she would learn, and she would do something else. That is a part of having 'IT.'

I think the other thing that I noticed, and this could be my preference, the common theme of people that have IT or sparkle is that I think they often don't know they do. There is a high level of humility in people with sparkle, that they're stunned when you say things to them like, 'Do you know the impact that you have on people?' They're like, 'Really?' Because I talked to her about it later and said, 'I just want you to know that all of these people who came up to me to talk afterwards, they had such endearing comments about you.' She's like, 'Oh, that's really cool.' But she had no idea.

The other thing is that humility part, is that they always put someone else out front first, that they don't crave that center of attention. And that they allow other people to shine, which I think builds a stronger community because of it. It actually makes them even more endearing that they share the stage.

I have another . . . example. During that trip, one of those gentlemen gave a passionate and heart-warming speech. It truly was remarkable. After he was done, I complimented him on it. He said, 'You can compliment [her]. I told her my story and what I wanted the audience to hear. I could have never put together such a well-written speech on my own.' [She] allowed him to shine and never once thought about taking credit for that speech. In fact, when I told her how much I enjoyed the speech, she took it in stride like it was an everyday occurrence. That's what I meant when I said what often makes highfliers special, is that they act with humility. They lift others who may not normally be the center of attention. Perhaps they are so often the center of attention that they relish the chance to witness others experience the joy and sense of accomplishment of being a highflier too."

You can easily see in reading all of these interview excerpts throughout the book how fortunate I have been to work with people like Marilyn and all the others. The TNTs that follow are a combination of suggestions about your messages and about your voice. There is so much you have in your power to project the kind of personality Marilyn is talking about. Now the TNTs:

- Telling yourself, "I love what I do and they need to hear it."

- Projecting optimism by predicting positive outcomes if we all work together. Reread that quote: "She makes me feel differently about the future than I used to feel."

- Giving credit to everyone but yourself. It's the work of others to give you credit. That is the definition of "humility."

- When Marilyn says, "She helped them get past their indignance about the way things are compared to how they think they should be," it suggests saying, "I know how you feel. So many others in this room agree with you. I just want to lay out some alternatives." (This is an example of Feel, Felt, and Found.)

- The thought that some people "stimulate inspiration in the people around them by their presence, and by their enthusiasm and their passion" suggests a stronger and enthusiastic voice to come across as, "I'm not just saying this. I feel every word of it."

- "She projects fearlessness." Simpler wording in your opinions sounds less cautious and less worried about the impressions left. I encourage you to express yourself with words like, "We have a real shot at making this happen" vs. "There's a potential positive outcome that could change our strategy if we are careful in how we proceed."

Showing Authentic Interest in Others

I interviewed Captain Samson Stevens, Sr. He is Chief of Atlantic Area Intelligence for the United States Coast Guard. I met him when I was asked to speak at the Naval Postgraduate School Center for Homeland Defense and Security Executive Leaders Program. He has 29 years of experience in a broad array of operational intelligence, joint and staff assignments that include Coast Guard Cutter MALLOW, the National Drug Intelligence Center, Coast Guard Headquarters Office of Design and Engineering Standards, and Office of Standards Evaluation and Development. He has been a Liaison Officer to the U.S. Fleet Forces Command and Joint Staff and the Executive Officer, Maritime Intelligence Fusion Center Pacific.

Captain Stevens graduated from the U.S. Coast Guard Academy in 1995 with a BS degree in Mechanical Engineering. He earned an MS degree in Kinesiology from the University of Michigan. He also has an MA degree in National Security and Strategic Studies from the U.S. Naval War College in 2011.

Captain Stevens shared this with me:

> *"I composed a list of people. There are people I saw as high-fliers or destined to be, and they share similar characteristics. The one I'm thinking of had a passion and fulfillment in work and it naturally brings people to them. People like them are genuine, sincere, and authentic in looking to their right and to their left and saying, 'This is my most important job and it's the people who are with me who I will invest the effort in.' They see someone who might be making copies or creating a binder and say something like, 'Hey, I haven't seen you in a while. I remember you were going on a softball trip and your son had just gotten a hit.'*

They make the effort to recall a personal tidbit of that person's life. I could tell it wasn't pro forma but done because they genuinely care and make those transactional leadership elements that are required in the business we must do. There's this full spectrum of interpersonal relationships that I think they build that at the end of the day means trust and builds a connectedness within an organizational unit that is supportive of people. And that's being that person who is invested in others.

So let me stop there because I could go on, anecdote or otherwise, of the qualities that people like that are related to their personality. And I think this is even more critical, post COVID, where virtual and online and telework venues have created the ability to be very transactional and very hyper efficient. There's a meeting, a five-minute break, and another meeting. It's 'Okay, let's get to business.' I feel like we've seen an inverse relationship to the necessary stock that we put in some of those skills. But this highflier did not fall into that trap."

Captain Stevens added some very interesting observations that I want to include here even though they were about an officer who had been around for a long time—someone who had most certainly been a highflier and grew into the role.

"I remember being in Alameda in 2013 to '16. There was a senior person who is always so busy with so much on his mind. But this person would always see me at the gym or wherever I was. Because my name is Sam, he would say, 'Hi Sam I am. How are you doing this morning?' And Allen, what he would do, if he was close enough, is he would just put a hand on the shoulder and remove it. I know there's a

whole science now about culture and touch. Is it too much, too long? Will it be creepy or not? And I have these issues come up in leadership circle discussions. I still use it to this day. If someone does a good job, this is their shoulder. 'Hey, good job.' And I'm done. But I want them to know that I'm present because I felt so connected by this person just right there. Firm and done. I might say, 'How are you? How's Kathy and the kids?' Even though a million things happened in this person's life that day.

The other one was about two years ago, a different person. It is another senior person but the same qualities are a part of the highflier I have in mind. This person was our former commandant. It was about two years before his change of command. He was presiding over a retirement ceremony, and I had known him for the past 10 years. He was very helpful in my career in terms of mentoring. He always remembered my kids' names, my family's names, and took time to mentor me and provide me career counsel.

The situation I'm remembering was a major social function and he was being swarmed by all the people who, of course, want to see a 'four star.' I was on my way out of the reception area and he saw me and made eye contact and said, 'Sam, come here for a sec.' He looked at me and interrupted his conversation and brought me in. When I came in, he put his hand on my left shoulder and said, 'Hey, Sam, let me just finish this conversation.' And then he brought me to his personal space, turned to me and said, 'It was good talking to you. Do you still have that Subaru? How's Kathy?' And of all the things that he had in his mind after having so many conversations that morning, he remembered these little things.

Those two pieces for me, Allen, just reflect a sincerity and authenticity and the physical element of leadership that I sometimes think we could probably give people more tools on. I don't want it to be, 'Oh, okay, put hand on shoulder and say, good job but not more than two seconds or less than one.' Of course it must be genuine. That takes me back to the highflier I've had in mind since we started talking. They constantly incorporate and read and acquire skills. They are curious and sincere and want to be better every day."

Captain Stevens could have been my coauthor given the TNTs related to personality that he offered in thinking about both a highflier early in their career and a Four Star Admiral. Let's review them:

- Stop in the middle of a task and turn your attention to a team member. That signals that personal relationships are the priority.

- Mention a personal detail about someone's life that signals how well you've listened over the time you've worked together.

- Pay special attention to what Captain Stevens said about virtual calls. Don't sacrifice the personal touch simply to be more efficient. Here's the example from above: "'Do you still have that Subaru? How's Kathy?' And of all the things that he had in his mind after having so many conversations that morning, he remembered these little things."

- The lesson about touch (it's called haptics) is to make it crisp and short. Captain Stevens used the shoulder as an example.

- Continue to be a reader and observer of "tips and tools" (like the book you're reading) to hone your skills. Sincerity and authenticity will emerge from practiced behavior.

Connecting with People in Admirable Ways

I interviewed Eric Hunter, the CEO of CareOregon. He spoke directly to highfliers' ability to connect with others. Since joining CareOregon in 2016, Eric has led its transformation into a community benefit organization with programs and reinvestments that support members and communities. Key priorities include behavioral health access, housing and food support, provider network growth, and the development of the health care workforce.

Before joining CareOregon, Eric held several executive leadership roles including Chief Operating Officer for Boston Medical Center HealthNet Plan, regional CEO for Value Options Behavioral Health (now part of Carelon Behavioral Health) in Texas and Illinois, and as CEO of Heartland Health Plan in Oklahoma. Eric also held senior positions at Schaller Anderson and Centene. Eric's state government experience includes positions in the Oklahoma Governor's Office and with the Oklahoma Health Care Authority.

Here's what Eric had to say:

"There are a few people who come to mind as you ask about the qualities of highfliers. Two of them stand out. After doing this work for 30 years now, there are some of them who far surpass a lot of other very talented people. I've been successful probably because of things that I saw coming. But the highflier I have in mind could connect with people in ways I can't imagine myself doing. I am not a particularly gregarious guy. I believe I am known for taking care of business. But this highflier went out of his way to get to know people and understand what made them tick. The connection he made with others allowed them a chance to offer valuable insights that he didn't have to ask for. That information fed into his knowledge base and skill

sets. I knew from the get-go that the way he engaged with people and made them feel allowed them to talk knowing that he really cared about what they were offering in the way of ideas. Watching him made me think, 'I really have to try harder to do what he does.' It was so natural for him. All of us have to work hard and often have to work hard on this connectivity issue. But I thought to myself, 'He's going to be a star.'

Another person who I knew was going to do good things was a person that worked for me in Indiana. This was another highflier who had the same ability to connect and communicate at the level of whomever they were talking to. Whether it was FQHC leaders in the community or corporate CEOs or customer service reps, they could connect at any level. People were never made to feel that this person was above or beneath them but always on par. This talent has been leveraged and now he is a regional VP and I am so proud of what they've been able to achieve. Humbly, I think I am as smart or smarter than some of the people with this ability to connect. There is simply a way to deal with people that is so underestimated. There are senior people who can get away with being a weirdo of sorts because they are the boss. But these two highfliers earned their way to the top through smarts and ability to connect."

TNTs growing out of this interview:

- Even in an enthusiastic back-and-forth conversation, do your level best not to interrupt. Show you are hanging on every word.

- Ask questions that look for more details as the conversation continues. "What dish did your mom or dad know was your favorite and it was waiting for you when you came home for the holidays? That's so interesting. What did your mom add to the recipe? Do you still make it yourself?"

- If you look at synonyms for "connect" you'll see "combine" and "unite." Think of the comments and questions you ask as intending to make those things happen.

Attracting the Smiles of Others

Dr. Ilan Shapiro came as close to describing charisma and personality as anyone I've interviewed and the role it plays in the highflier puzzle. First, some background on him. Dr. Shapiro is the Chief Health Correspondent and Medical Affairs Officer at AltaMed Health Services. In addition to being a practicing physician, Dr. Shapiro is actively involved in creating binational public health programs to reach Hispanic communities on both sides of the border. He acted as the Medical Advisor for the General Consulate of Mexico in Chicago and was a Member of the Editorial Board for A Tu Salud (For Your Health), a health bulletin representing Hispanic health topics and resources. Dr. Shapiro is part of the National Hispanic Medical Association and a spokesperson for the American Academy of Pediatrics. Dr. Shapiro earned a medical degree from Anahuac University in Mexico, and had the opportunity to practice medicine in several main hospitals in Mexico and has been serving in federally qualified health clinics in Chicago, Fort Myers (Florida), and Los Angeles. (I cannot believe the good fortune bestowed on me in the quality of clients I have had the pleasure to serve.)

Dr. Shapiro said, "When you go to a room and you have someone, this person I am thinking of, that has light upon them. That is how I would describe it. People smile at them without knowing who they are. This is that person. They not only understand the importance of creating balanced conversation with people, hearing them and all that goes with that, but do all that while working to become the Director of a hospital here in Los Angeles."

Before I continue Dr. Shapiro's comments, I want you to read something very much related to his feeling of meeting this person. I recently bought a book about celebrity political candidates. The author writes, "I ask people exactly what they think makes a celebrity a celebrity. 'It's the feeling you get when someone famous is in the room, like chills. It's not like being in the company of normal people. Their eyes are brighter.' ... Another man said, 'and their smiles are whiter. They make you feel special.'" (Wright 2020)

Dr. Shapiro continued:

"I met him at a very early stage in his career. It was 20 years ago they were finishing the program in internal medicine. He progressed quickly in his career because it was clear that he, first and foremost, knew how to take responsibility.

Even though I was a student, and he was finishing the program, he was actually acting the role and the position. He opened the doors for me at every chance that he had. And he became a connector. He was well liked. His focus was not only on his job. It was also making sure that he created a lot of peripheral things that are not the 'Classic Doctor' things. He was making sure that he created a group and treated me personally as my mentor. He eventually was one of the co-founders to bring more Hispano students and to have a pipeline to get to med school. And that was with very high volume and very high demanding job. But he still managed to open all these things and being humble, honest and being present.

Right now, I have the joy of working with him. He is probably a couple years older than me at this point. I was finishing my residency, and he already had a couple years practicing. He was at such a young age in his career. He was offered to be a Director of Internal Medicine at a hospital. And today I have the pleasure to work with him. I have seen how he went to all these places because I saw the highflier qualities at the start. He went to Sacramento but whoever you mention his name to, it is as if you were watching a movie and someone actually mentions the name of someone and everybody gets it. With him it's 'The Light.' There's his smile and that goes with the amazing work. But they always have a story about how he helped someone or how he was involved in some work product or the space that he created for them. So it was always a pleasure to work with him.

And the thing that I cherish about him a lot is the consistency in his behavior. I have seen, and we all have, I have seen people that climb the ladder, and they start forgetting things. They forget, seemingly, the values they had earlier or the actions like smiling and being human. Because of their responsibilities, the stress, or whatever excuse we have … they forget. But he continued to be true to himself. Yes, he has less time to actually do a lot of the things that he used to, but he's still there and when I know that if I need to call him right now, he will pick up the phone. And that is certainly not because I am 'important.' It is because he wants to continue to create that space."

Here are the TNTs that emerge from Dr. Shapiro's interview. And let me first say that for as long as any of us can remember, it has been a mantra that "you cannot bottle charisma." It is no different than those who say, "You cannot teach sales skills. You either have it or you don't." It's a depressing thought if true and all the publishers of self-help books would have to shrug their combined shoulders and stop marketing those books. So I am going to review what Dr. Shapiro told me in this interview that we can add to what has already been said about the "It Factor."

- "This person I am thinking of has a light upon them." When you are at a gathering of people, there is a saying in communication studies that "you cannot *not* communicate." I encourage you to not stand still with your hands at your side even when you are not talking. The same goes for when you are sitting. Keep your hands on the table or, if no table, keep them in your lap. Your eyes need to look alert to what is around you so that you are not observed as staring. If there is art on the wall, walk toward a few pieces and look at them in a way that brings others to them because you look so interested.

- "They not only understand the importance of creating balanced conversation with people, hearing them and all that goes with that, but do all that while working to become the Director of a hospital here in Los Angeles." If you are talking to one person or a small group gathered together, your interest in what others are saying should be palpable. I have talked about this for many years as recognizing the difference between the teacher in you and the student in you. Dr. Shapiro is remarking on the way this highflier came across as an interested and enthusiastic student as others were talking with or to each other. The "char" that is the prefix to **char**isma, **char**acter and **char**m translates to top notch listening.

- Dr. Shapiro's words in the previous bullet are worth using again to illustrate a different point: There is a term that you might think of as synonymous with fake, false, and inauthentic. That word is flattery. When Dr. Shapiro talks about a balanced conversation, he is referring to the feeling others get that you have a balanced view about what they are expressing. When you genuinely say, "That is so interesting. I haven't heard it expressed quite that way. Tell me more," you are expressing that you seek a balanced view and that you think this conversation partner can give it to you. For so many who might be taking a risk expressing themselves, it is flattering to hear the receiver commenting that way. Google distinguishes flattery from praise and reminds us to be careful with flattery for fear that it will sound insincere. I am 100 percent in agreement.

- A "balanced" conversation means that you can talk about topics that others bring up. The TNT here is to be fairly well read on a lot of topics that come up when people gather. I have continually urged my clients to be "three paragraphs deep" on just about everything. I have pushed this idea by encouraging you to think of yourself as the sections of, yes, the old-fashioned newspaper. International news: you should know the headlines. National news, Entertainment, Style, Sports, and even Geography ... know the headlines. Recently someone at a gathering after a seminar was talking about where he went to college. He said it was a school I probably would not know about. "Try me," I said. He said, "It's the second largest university in the state system." I said, "Mankato." He was delighted.

Chapter 8

Unlimited Effort

*I was impressed with how hard they pushed for results for them-
selves and the team. They showed so much energy and effort!*

When the time came to choose a topic for my PhD dissertation,
I decided to veer substantially from all the research and course
work up to that time. My focus had always been on attitude change
and persuasion. (And as you can see, I cover that substantially in
Chapter 10.) I decided to do a scientifically based study of friendship formation. Based on the research already done, I posited several
hypotheses, including a couple based on similarity of personality and
another one based on the type of question-asking the studied dyads
(couples) used when talking with each other.

There's a standard conclusion all of these studies have that
looks like this: "Each problem observed in the present study has an
implication for further study," or "This is a fruitful area to pursue in
future research." One conclusion, however, paid off. There was clear
evidence that the studied couples felt that the more effort a person
showed to become a friend was a predictor of success.

And that word, "effort," is at the heart of the research and interviews
you will see in this chapter on the power of energy and drive, which
has come to be called *passion*, to be seen as a highflier. (Parenthetically,
I read recently that essay reviewers at Ivy League universities have been
turned off by the word *passion*. Personally, I prefer *effort*.)

Energy Translates to Effort

A part of my foundation for pushing you in this direction is my personal experience as a young consultant just beginning my career. Once I saw some success scheduling seminars and workshops and giving one-to-one advice to people who wanted tips on communication, I immediately was receiving post-program evaluations … lots and lots of them. The surveys produced by the hosts were directed primarily at the usefulness of my advice. There were items such as "Did you find the facilitator's comments and advice tailored to your work?" There might have been a question like, "Did the facilitator help maintain your interest throughout the day?" Thankfully, my evaluations were good, and I was asked to do more of these programs.

But there was also room for open-ended comments. And those were the most revealing parts of the evaluation process. Over and over, I was complimented for my effort and energy level. I felt obligated to keep them energized throughout a full day, and my behavior showed it. I was always louder than was necessary to be heard. My volume was a sign of the effort I was putting in. I wanted people to say, "He puts so much effort in to make us feel the material was important." The content had to stand on its own. But my manner could not be ignored.

So, first some research on this issue to support my personal experience and what I'm guessing is your experience as well.

Passion Appreciates Passion

Jon M. Jachimowicz, Andreas Wihler, and Adam D. Galinsky wrote about passion and performance reviews in 2020. The executive summary included this: "Companies often celebrate employees who successfully pursue their passion. Academic research suggests that these positive evaluations occur because of the passion percolating inside the employee. We propose that supervisors are also a key piece of this puzzle: Supervisors who are more successful in their own pursuit of passion place more value on passion in their performance evaluations. This produces an interpersonal dynamic whereby employees who are more successful in pursuing their passion may receive higher performance ratings when their supervisors are also more successful in pursing their own passion." (Jachimowicz, Wihler, and Galinsky 2020)

After citing their research process, the authors write, "We demonstrate that this interpersonal dynamic is specific to passion and does not apply to less observable motivations (intrinsic and extrinsic motivation). These results demonstrate that supervisors who successfully pursue their passion may overvalue passion relative to other attributes, leading to potential bias."

The TNT associated with that comment comes down, once again, to the truism that the person evaluating you uses themselves as a standard for what is expected of you. In simpler words, similarity in personal style is a better predictor of satisfying evaluations than a major difference in style. Passion appreciates passion. Introversion appreciates introversion. Workhorse appreciates workhorse.

Passion Implies Higher Performance Ratings

In their introduction to their article on passion, Jon M. Jachimowicz, Andreas Wihler, and Adam D. Galinsky claim that companies are putting more emphasis on exhibited passion for work. "Firms shape their hiring practices to attract candidates who wish to pursue their passion, develop procedures to help their employees successfully fulfill their passion, and fire employees who are no longer passionate for their work (Bolles 2009; Duckworth 2016; Isaacson 2011; Wolf et al. 2016). As a result, employees increasingly value the pursuit of passion for work, in part with the hope of attaining higher levels of job performance (O'Keefe et al. 2018)." (Jachimowicz, Wihler, and Galinsky 2020)

Clearly, this all begs the questions, "What do people do that shows passion for their work? How do others know how much they value the job they have?"

Your attitude and effort are going to be noticed, and you will see that in some of the interviews I conducted with people whose job it is to spot highfliers. Here's another example: I had a one-hour client meeting just a few days ago. He told me he had a series of year-end reviews with five senior people in the company. The only issue that came up for his consideration was a feeling that he was not participating in meetings in a way that showed sufficient interest.

Even in our meetings I thought he was somewhat nonplussed. That means he did not seem to be looking to use me as a helper. He sat quietly, did not take notes, did not ask any questions. The way clients act with me is not always a reflection of the way they act with their colleagues, but I can't ignore the possibility that it is. I am obligated to put great effort into client meetings. I must prepare for them and orchestrate them in a way that my client feels I am worth the fee.

I told him that if he imagined himself as a consultant brought into the company to offer his advice, his instincts would direct him to show more interest and intent to help when he sat with them. Otherwise they would find someone else.

Styles That Complement Each Other

I never fail to give credit to Deborah Tannen for helping women think about communication at work. And her take is an especially timely perspective given a chapter on effort and energy. But first, who's Deborah Tannen? Here is an abridged biography. She is a Distinguished University Professor in the Linguistics Department at Georgetown University and author of many books and articles about how the language of everyday conversation affects relationships. Her book *You Just Don't Understand: Women and Men in Conversation* was on The *New York Times* best seller list for nearly four years, including eight months as No. 1, and has been translated into 31 languages. This is the book that brought gender differences in communication style to the forefront of public awareness. *Talking from 9 to 5: Women and Men at Work* was a *New York Times Business* best seller. She has been featured in and has written for most major newspapers and magazines, including *The New York Times*, *The Washington Post*, *The Atlantic*, *HuffPost*, *Newsweek*, *Time*, *USA Today*, *People*, and *The Harvard Business Review*.

Tannen makes the case, as I wrote about earlier, that "people in powerful positions are likely to reward styles similar to their own." She goes on to say that people who are fine with speaking up in front of others do not wait for silence to get heard: "It's common to observe women who participate actively in one-on-one discussions or in all-female groups but who are seldom heard in meetings with a large proportion of men. On the other hand, there are women who share the style more common among men, and they run a different risk—of being seen as too aggressive." Finally, she writes, "As the workplace becomes more culturally diverse and business becomes more global, managers will need to become even better at reading interactions and more flexible in adjusting their own styles to the people with whom they interact." (Tannen 1995)

And that brings us right back to the effort it takes to be a highflier. If you are going to read interactions in the room, I want you to have detective skills that few have. And that takes effort. You need to be so much more conscious of what is going on around you, and that is not "relaxing." You must have better ears and eyes as you hear and see what people are saying and how they are saying it.

I also have some things to say about the effort some senior people feel you need to exert when you come to work *if* you make the effort to go to the actual workplace. These last few years almost all my corporate clients have offered what many Gen Z employees have called "work–life balance." So many of the senior people Gen Z employees report to are ambivalent about the concept.

Here's an example from a recent piece in *The Wall Street Journal's* Business section. Eric Schmidt, ex-CEO and executive chairman at Google, says his former company is losing the artificial intelligence race and remote work is to blame. "Google decided that work-life balance and going home early was more important than winning. And the reason the startups work is because the people work like hell." Schmidt made the comments in a discussion at Stanford. His remarks about Google's remote-work policies were in response to a question about Google competing with OpenAI.

He joins a long list of corporate leaders, including JP Morgan Chase CEO Jamie Dimon and Tesla CEO Elon Musk, who have complained about work-from-home policies, saying they make companies less efficient and less competitive. Dimon said in an annual letter a few years ago that people in the upper ranks "cannot lead from behind a desk or in front of a screen." Musk has said workers need "a minimum of 40 hours in the office per week." (De Avila 2024)

I am not a McKinsey or Bain consultant with a vital interest in Google's competitiveness. I am only interested in your reputation as a highflier related to how much effort you seem to display with your work. If your boss was Jamie Dimon, he would pay attention to your work ethic. And I cannot rest if I ignore his message here and how judgments about you are partially based on this.

Adjusting Energy Level to the Setting

It may appear at first read that I have a bias toward maximum effort or energy displayed all the time. I interviewed Chris Kendall for a more balanced view. Chris was a highflier himself when we first met nearly

20 years ago when he was at Noble Energy in Houston. He was the President and Chief Executive Officer of Denbury, Inc., and he also served as a member of Denbury's Board of Directors until Denbury was acquired by Exxon in 2023. Prior to Denbury, while at Noble Energy, he held a wide range of international and domestic leadership positions, primarily in the Eastern Mediterranean, Latin America, and the Gulf of Mexico regions. Chris earned his Bachelor of Science degree in Engineering, Civil Specialty, from the Colorado School of Mines and is a graduate of the Advanced Management Program at the Harvard Business School. He is also a member of the National Petroleum Council.

I worked with Chris preparing for an earnings call during his Noble days. I gave him TNTs for both the messaging and the delivery. A few weeks later, when he walked into our next planned session, he gave me a high five. He told me that one of the attendees sitting next to Chuck Davidson (who I introduce in Chapter 6) at that meeting said, "Now I see the kind of leaders you've developed here." All of us who do this kind of advice giving yearn for feedback—complimentary feedback, of course—about our suggestions. Chris's comment was enough to energize me for the rest of the day. It was evidence that one event, one presentation in this case, can be enough to generate a response like "the kind of leaders you've developed."

Here is what Chris had to say about the highflier who he singled out for praise in our interview. It is a description of someone who could, on demand, gauge the effort needed depending on the circumstance.

"The gentleman I'm talking about ... could change his energy level. I remember both presentations and small group conversations. He could match the energy level of a board compared to the level of energy in, say, a town hall. He had the ability to adapt to situations as different

as those. You do not see that very often. You generally see people who have a certain way about them, and it comes out no matter what situation they are in. With a board, a high level of energy could come across as too enthusiastic and not realistic. A board often has a lower level of energy that appears thoughtful and considerate in the true sense of the word as defining 'considering different things.' They want to be considerate of the whole situation under discussion.

He left sufficient pauses between his thoughts to give board members a moment to think. When he was talking to employees in a town hall, he knew they had to be motivated and fired up and ready to take the next hill. And he was a natural at that … a master. And he was only in his 30s. It was something I noted as a fundamental difference maker for him.

Now he was really smart. Allen, you have met many Denbury employees. We have so many smart people. But his ability to communicate in that way, and to be thoughtful, was quite stunning. He was someone who was determined to use tools he had learned in sessions like the ones I had with you. Regardless of the situation, he could communicate thoughtfulness, not just information. You could see how he considered the questions he was asked in the context of the message he was trying to convey. And I was struck by his ability to do that. I had the gift of so many employees I could watch in different settings and how they would handle a similar situation."

I included Chris's interview in this chapter because of the emphasis on putting in sufficient effort in preparation to raise and lower energy level depending on the listener(s). Chris feels that most people have a way of coming across that every listener sees and hears. It certainly is a lot easier that way. That is where the expression "just relax and be yourself" comes from. It takes work, it takes serious thinking, to alter your fallback communication style.

The first TNT I want you to practice is placing longer pauses between sentences. The longer the pause, the more emphasis you want your listener to give to what you have just said. Hopefully, the content justifies the pause. But even if it is not an earth-shaking thought you have uttered, the pause makes it seem so. It is as if you are saying to the board, "Consider this."

Another TNT addresses Chris's comment about answering questions in the context of the message he wanted to get across. Questioners often do not realize how hard it is to address their question given the way it was asked. Imagine this one: "I am having a problem understanding exactly what you are trying to say. Are you suggesting we move forward before the end of the year because that seems risky to me given our other priorities that you seem to be ignoring, so I am bewildered about some of your thoughts here. Have you had a chance to go over this proposal with other members of the Senior Leadership Team?" The question, as put, is a combination of statements and questions. If you hear the actual questions, and think about the feeling behind the words and respond to it, I will want you to answer by saying, "I think the outcome is worth the emphasis I am putting on scheduling this. [pause] I have had a chance to pass the idea through the SLT."

As to the compliment about the effort it takes to raise and lower the temperature, so to speak, given the different audiences, the style of high energy always means faster and louder and fewer pauses. It's characterized by sentences after sentence with barely a chance to think about any of them. It is so common for people praising the style in a high energy motivational presentation to say, "I don't remember exactly what they said, but I just know I am ready to take that hill." Lower energy is softer and slower. Think about it: It's the difference between a hard-driving rock song and a romantic ballad.

Perpetual Restlessness

Greg Sills is a client I've known since the mid-1980s and watched as he evolved into a highly respected expert on leading projects. Here is a bit about Greg's background: As President of consulting firm Leading Projects LLC, he recently served as Executive Advisor and Chief Transformation Officer for the CEO of a European oil and gas company. He provides executive advisory services in the oil and gas, chemicals, mining, and power industries. Greg has more than 35 years of experience managing major projects, engineering, and operational excellence around the world, and creating systems to make high performance repeatable.

Greg was Executive Vice President and Chief Development Officer at Cobalt International Energy, with global accountability for bringing deepwater discoveries through the development pipeline and into production. Prior to his position at Cobalt, Greg served as Vice President, Upstream Developments at Marathon Oil. Before joining Marathon, Greg served as Vice President, Major Projects for BP. As VP of Major Projects, Greg stewarded the development and curriculum of BP's two major learning platforms.

Greg began describing a highflier he first saw in a presentation. He then elaborated by describing behavior that reflects the tone of this chapter, which is energy produced through effort.

> *"I first heard an opening that showed confidence. It was more than just an attention grabber. It was relevant to the topic. It got all of us in the audience to sit up straight and focus on them. When the questions came, it was*

*clear they had anticipated and had prepared by think-
ing about appropriate responses. If there was data on
a slide, the words I heard were, 'Looking at these numbers, a question you might have is...' It was done in a
way that did not come across as trying to cut someone
off but a way to show they had thought about the data
beyond the typical view. And that brings me to the issue
of effort. Highfliers are known for delivering more than
people expected. You can call it hardworking, but it is a
clear way of showing a personal drive and aspirations
that surprise your boss."*

It was at this point in the interview that Greg introduced me to a
new concept: perpetual restlessness. It is a sign of extra effort even
in a "quiet period."

*"This person had one of my pet qualities and that was agility
or nimbleness when it comes to managing the unexpected.
It's a muscle that's underdeveloped. A lot of people are pre-
occupied with failure. In other words, they obsess over the
smallest errors and deviations from previous expectations.
And that is how incidents are headed off. The person I am
thinking of, and there have been a few of them, has this
perpetual restlessness when they are in a quiet period. They
do not take the idea of 'no news is good news.' To them
it is just no news. In fact, it may be bad news and they
ask themselves if they have not listened hard enough. That
restlessness opens their ears a little bit to what I think of as
'faint signals' of deviations from expectations. It goes hand
in hand with anticipating things in a presentation. It is all
variations of the same muscle."*

So what are some TNTs?

- In a "quiet" period, make sure colleagues can see your concentration.
- Ask questions, the answers to which get something to the next level.

Off and Running

The last interview I conducted about effort and energy was with Mike Baird. He has an impressive background. He served as CEO for Henry Schein One, the world leader in dental practice management software. HS1 offers market-leading solutions for dental practices, including Dentrix, Ascend, Dentrix Enterprise, Easy Dental, TechCentral, Demandforce, Lighthouse360, Officite, and DentalPlans.com as well as leading practice solutions in 12 countries.

Prior to Henry Schein One, he was founder and CEO of Avizia and served as President of Amwell after Avizia was acquired in 2018. Previously, he held senior positions at Tandberg, Cisco, McKinsey & Company, and Dell. Mike serves on the board of the American Telemedicine Association and is a Venture Partner at Waterline Ventures.

Mike holds a BS degree in accounting from Brigham Young University, an MBA with distinction from the Kellogg School of Management at Northwestern University, and was designated in 2005 as a Siebel Scholar.

Mike began by saying the following:

> *"The first thing I thought about after your email was this: There's a term in the military called fire and forget. You don't have to worry about missiles because they auto track. I'm going to call it 'line up and go right.' It's the notion that people, at an early age, can have a task explained to*

them and they're off to do it. They don't need a lot of guidance. They can just take a big responsibility on and just jump after it. Obviously, they're good when they come back and get little corrections. Sometimes they can go way off in the wrong direction, but I love that they are quick, capture things in a moment and they are off and running. And you just instantly trust them and what they are willing to do. That is at the heart of the highflier I have in mind.

The second point is they were always willing to take on more. They have capacity that is seemingly endless. This highflier figured out how to organize and structure. They have energy and work incredibly hard but they have this ability to cram a lot of things in. I gave them more and more to do, and that drove their acceleration in the organization even faster. They were always the first one to say 'I will do that.'

In addition, they are not constrained by prior experience. I mean that if we were in a brainstorming meeting and someone brings up an idea that we had seen somewhere in our history, we would be much quicker to say, 'No, that's not going to work. We've tried it before. It didn't work.' This person wasn't going to be constrained by that. They don't dismiss something that quickly. They would say, 'Let's see what's different about this compared to what we are seeing now.' A highflier, especially someone new, is not going to be held back by that.

One example involved AI. We had tried it six years ago and it was garbage. But the highflier came in and said, 'No. Have you seen what is out there now? Things are changing by the minute.' Eight percent of the time I may get an answer right because of the things I've messed up in the past. But what about the 20 percent when I needed that extra voice? These are the highfliers I love. They came to a meeting unconstrained. They are the best thought partners. I loved going to the white board together. This one was an idea factory. Two out of three might be bad but maybe just in this moment in time. They throw new stuff out there and there was a freshness to it. There is a drive for innovation backed by a lot of creativity. And, for sure, a willingness to take risks. Other people may have learned the politics of an organization. They've learned what gets their hands slapped. They think, 'If I just operate in this perfect range, I'm going to do good enough and I won't get my hands slapped. Just stay under the radar.' Yeah, they do wrong things sometimes and we have to teach them how to communicate. And they may offend someone now and then. But this highflier was someone who might misfire but brings so much energy and drive and ambition, and who wants 'it' really bad."

Mike added even more:

"There's something about managing discouragement and things of that nature. There's a resilience there. They are bringing new ideas about various things people bring up a lot. Some people just say, 'I should stop.' But the highfliers are the ones who are just like, 'It's whack a mole.' They keep putting their head up again. They are going to get bopped on some things, but because they're willing to put themselves out there and do it over and over again, they are going to get the breakthrough idea at some point that is ahead of their years. They're willing to and that's why they are the ones who break through the organization. It's not that they didn't say something stupid. Eventually they will come up with an idea. That's your passion. Someone like me will say, 'OK, I'm going to give you the chance to run

with it.' That's why they break through. They get that special project. Yeah, you're still an analyst, a first-year consultant. But because you pushed and you drove, you eventually overcame the odds. You got that one extra tilt, that one little extra project or assignment or visibility point or meeting or whatever it is you run with. Because you persisted, and you have that success, when I sit down at the end of the year and I'm evaluating my teams, you did this one thing that really sticks out to me that was above and beyond everybody else. That's where you really start to see him or her.

So what happens the next year? You elevate them a little bit. They get more scope and range. They get more exposure to executives. That knocks some of the hard edges off. They get preferential treatment in a way. They get two or three special projects because they are more trusted. They took those extra lumps and ended up getting that little side thing and somehow, they manage, that when everyone else gets 100 things done, they get 101 and the right to be built up and put ahead. That's how I would describe it."

Mike's interview is a perfect conclusion to this chapter about effort. I began with a high-level reminder about how it played into my dissertation. Mike takes that into an extremely helpful detailed explanation about how it plays out in your day-to-day at work. Noticeable effort will be rewarded.

Get ready for the TNTs:

- Saying "I'll give that a shot" or "Our team can take that on" builds trust.

- Your demonstration of structure and organization is a stress reducer for your boss.

- Avoid saying, "We tried that in my prior job and it didn't work."

Chapter 9

Born or Made Leaders: "Organic" or "Preservatives Added"

Whether born or made, and I don't care which, team members gravitated toward them.

There are so many instances in my practice when I was asked to give suggestions about how to have conversations about performance, which are not something any of us look forward to as we drive to work. In addition, I began some years ago saying this to seminar participants: "Part of every day, I want you to think of yourself as a teacher and the other part of that same day as a student. The 'teacher in you' speaks up at meetings and makes presentations and offers advice and suggestions. That's mentoring. The 'student in you' listens and asks questions as others do the same thing."

But then I realized that a responsible approach means I must do a "root cause" analysis, so to speak, about the qualities in some of us that invite others to seek our feedback and to seek our guidance as mentors long before we are formally recognized as leaders and given senior positions. What draws us to some people? What magnetic force makes that happen? Are you born with that force, or can you develop it?

As always, in this chapter I will lead with a bit of communication research, report on what my interviewees—leaders themselves—said about these "born leaders," and leave you with tips and tools (those TNTs).

Born with, or Developed with Experience?

As a reminder, believe me, you do not get to shrug your shoulders and say, "Well, I guess I wasn't born with this special sauce so there's no reason to read further." Simply because some people are called "born leaders" does not imply that we are going to minimize all that is nurtured in us as we begin life's journey. Keep reading for some interesting research on born leadership versus made leadership.

Leaders Showing "Born With" Traits Build Trust Early

In an excellent piece by the Indeed Editorial Team, they report, "A born leader may be predisposed to success, but everyone can learn to improve their leadership skills. ... Born leaders are people with an innate capacity to effectively manage and lead groups of people to achieve collective goals. Instead of learning to become an effective leader, they have the instinctive ability to inspire others and encourage them to follow their vision. Employees feel more comfortable accepting instructions and trusting natural born leaders. Born leaders can continually improve their leadership by identifying new skills to develop and practicing different management styles." (Indeed, n.d.) The piece lists six qualities of a born leader:

- They find meaning and purpose in their work.
- They are great listeners (great "students").
- They don't overwork themselves.
- They constantly learn new things (more great "students").
- They have self-confidence.
- They unite employees.

The global notion about "born" and "made" can be food for thought about every quality in humans, including IQ, and much less the subjective label "leader." If there's one quality that some of us have early, maybe more than others, it is curiosity. The fact that you are reading this book is certainly one piece of evidence that you have it. Thank your ancestors or thank your powers of observation.

Presumed "Born With" Traits Can Be Learned

Hubert Joly lectures at Harvard Business School and was the CEO of Best Buy. Under the heading "Myth #2: People Are Born Leaders" in an article titled "The Case for Purposeful Leadership," he writes:

> *"When Lloyd Blankfein was still CEO of investment bank Goldman Sachs, I heard a speech he once gave at the Minneapolis Club. Blankfein shared with us that, every day while shaving, he asked himself, "Is it today? Is it today that the world is going to realize that I am not competent for this job?" Here was one of the most successful bankers in the world, and he was doubting his own abilities. Most leaders I know—myself included—suffer from the same imposter syndrome.*
>
> *That syndrome is born in part out of the misguided belief that leadership is an innate ability, emerging out of a level of intelligence, self-confidence, and charisma that you're born either with or without. If it were true, there would be just a few exceptional beings who could do the job, and the rest of us would be out of luck. Research suggests it's not true, though; so do the lives of great leaders.*
>
> *I believe that most of the attributes often associated with 'innate' leadership—from strategic thinking to eloquence—can be learned." (Joly and Lambert 2021)*

Whew. Relax. There you have it. "From strategic thinking to eloquence" are the anchors of a continuum reflecting competence to communication skill. I have already given you TNTs on critical thinking as well as strategic thinking. I have filled earlier chapters in this book with skills about speaking.

Leaders Have a Way of Inspiring Leadership Traits in Others

If you pay attention to the behaviors you see displayed every day, or that you hear about from others, you'll be part of an ongoing "class" in leadership. Pay special attention to communication style and even more specifically to the simplicity of the words that have a ring of truth to them.

For many years, I have encouraged my clients to read biographies of people they admire along with self-help books ... maybe even more so. Patti P. Phillips and Jack J. Phillips wrote, "John Quincy Adams, the sixth President of the United States, from 1825 to 1829, was quoted as saying, 'Successful leaders inspire others to learn more, do more, and become more.' This logic suggests varying levels of outcomes associated with leadership.

- Inspiring others means that leaders compel those who follow to feel or do something different. This reaction to the leader is the first level of success.

- Learning more means that people gain new knowledge or insight from the leader. Learning is the second level of success.

- Doing more means a leader drives change. They influence others to act, applying what they learn. Without action, the leader has little influence." (Phillips and Phillips 2023)

New TNTs for you based on these ideas:

- The pressure to maintain the status quo is immense. The change you suggest to someone must be marginal, not incremental.

- Bring data to the table that cannot be ignored. Statistics and quotes from recognized sources qualify as "new knowledge" and "new insights."

- "Do something different" and "driving change" are one and the same. Everything I've told you about problem solving requires an action step. I told a client just recently that giving critical feedback requires four lines: The issue. The consequences of the issue. The "do something different" and the benefits of that.

A Shift in the Research

Bradford R. Glaser did us the favor of writing a condensed history of natural vs. made leaders in a piece titled "Born Leader vs. Made Leader and the Difference Between Them." He wrote, "It wasn't until the 20th century that the perception of leadership skills being inherited at birth started to shift. Decades of research were prompted, in particular, by the writings of Thomas Carlyle and Francis Galton in the 19th century....Both Carlyle's *Heroes and Hero Worship* and Galton's *Hereditary Genius* contributed to initial support for the idea leaders are born rather than made." (Glaser 2023)

By the 1940s and 1950s, there was a shift in the research. People found that certain traits might come up in some situations but not in others. This was called the *situational approach* as opposed to personality traits and posited that it was behaviors rather than traits that resulted in effective results. Glaser writes, "Trait theory experienced a reemergence later in the 20th century thanks to improvements in methodology."

Studies revealed that people emerge as leaders as a result of various tasks and situations. They listed some traits:

- Conscientiousness
- Intelligence
- Adjustment
- General self-efficacy
- Extraversion
- Openness to experience

I loved a quote that Glaser included in his piece. Vince Lombardi (the coach of the Green Bay Packers championship professional football teams in the 1960s) said, "Leaders aren't born, they are made. And they are made just like anything else, through hard work." (Read Chapter 8 again!)

Even if it was accurate that leaders have some traits by birth, Glaser wrote that a study by the University of Illinois College of Agricultural, Consumer, and Environmental Sciences "found that leaders are, in fact, made and not born. This study suggests that leadership is ultimately 70% a result of lessons an individual learns through life experience and 30% genetic." The researchers wrote that "being ready and willing to learn how to be a leader is one of the most essential elements of developing leadership skills."

Glaser argues that psychologists are doubtful about the idea that people can be "predisposed to leadership because of inherited traits. One reason for the criticism is that people can possess these traits without being particularly inclined toward leadership or successful in their leadership endeavors." (Glaser 2023) Glaser goes on to say that what is called *contingency theory* makes the case that leaders adjust their behavior depending on context. So, it wouldn't be just a matter of having born-with traits. A leader's actions would also require looking at the needs of followers and the existing circumstances.

In addition, as you continue your study of leadership, you will find behavioral theories that suggest that leaders are 100 percent made. Behaviorists (like B.F. Skinner, whom I spoke about earlier in this book) believe that environmental conditioning determines actions. A highflier, in other words, watches, goes through an experience, and teachers others.

Leadership Qualities Can Be Seen Early in Childhood

Apropos our focus here on organic (born with) or preservatives added (learned skills), there is a terrific research piece done as a doctoral dissertation by Robin Sacks at the University of Toronto. Her aim was to find the core elements of leadership development in adolescents. Her work was titled "Natural Born Leaders: An Exploration of Leadership Development in Children and Adolescents." She developed four phases of leadership that she labeled "The Helper," "The Deputy," "The Agent," and "The Ambassador." I believe it's a fine way to look at highfliers and how they might be initially observed.

Sacks makes it clear that, in her opinion, there are differences between adult and adolescent leadership but "the dominant models of adult leadership ... often serve as the de-facto models of youth leadership." (Sacks 2009) Sacks explains that there was "a trait approach, which emphasized the personal attributes of leaders including intelligence, self-confidence, determination, integrity and sociability ... a behavioural approach ... Different patterns of behaviour were grouped together and labeled as styles ... The situational approach arose as researchers began to entertain the idea that leadership needs change from situation to situation ... The influence approach explains leadership in terms of the amount and type of power and how power is exercised."

In her results section, Sacks writes, "In each of the focus groups we asked, 'Can anyone be a leader?' and the students had a common response—'yes, but.'" The students understood that for leaders to emerge, they need opportunity and encouragement. The kids she asked said, "You need to be given opportunities to show that you are a leader." They "did not believe that some students were better suited than others to lead or influence an environment. Instead, their common view was that any student, when given the opportunity can be the leader." *Out of the mouths of babes* was my reaction to her results section.

Sacks also writes, "Comments about leaders were heavily weighted in terms of leadership characteristics such as optimism, perseverance and initiative. No students in any of the focus groups mentioned leadership skills like time management, project planning, and delegation. Even when we asked more pointedly about what leaders specifically do, students didn't mention leadership tasks or skills... The students responded, 'They take charge but not in a bossy way' and 'They respect themselves and their peers.'"

Here's the operative paragraph in my opinion: "This finding matches those discussed ... in the literature review." Those researchers "found that children appear to prioritize traits and personal qualities in their definitions of leadership. Adults also prioritize traits and personal qualities when defining leadership; however, adults appear to focus on different traits such as sense of purpose and consistency ... neither of which were mentioned by students."

All of this tells us that our take on what highfliers say and do starts early in childhood development and is sustained through adulthood. When you say to your boss, "I'll take that on," you are simply awakening a core belief in your boss about what leaders are supposed to do.

The Great Man Theory and the Big Five

I am actually pleased with my analogy as a chapter title, "organic or preservatives added." Those preservatives are in the form of mentoring and training. Highfliers will take to the lessons learned from others and from their reading and leadership training opportunities in such a way that no one will bat an eye as to how they came to be what they show themselves to be. I owe you a balanced take on this debate because I know without it, you could surmise where I fall on the continuum between agree and disagree. After all, I am a part of the training and development industry.

Have you been endowed with unique gifts and traits to earn what Thomas Carlyle called the "Great Man Theory"? If he was right, all of you deserve your advancement in the organization by nature. Now Carlyle would not have lasted as an "expert" in today's environment because, for one, he included traits like height as well as personality and intelligence.

The assumption behind Carlyle's ideas was that if you find a person with the right traits, that person can improve a team's performance and help it achieve its goals. For all of you who have been "accused of getting into the weeds," here's a dose to ponder.

"Numerous twin studies suggest that excellent leadership has a specific genetic basis. One study specifically showed a link between leadership role occupancy and the rs4950 genetic marker. This single nucleotide polymorphism is found on the neuronal acetylcholine receptor gene, which is associated with personality traits. Researchers suggest that those who possess this particular genetic marker are most likely to be successful and effective leaders.

The most influential leaders generally have an above-average level of intelligence. While anyone can gain intelligence through study and dedication, some research has also revealed that, to a certain extent, intelligence levels are inherited. A group of Glasgow-based researchers interviewed 12,686 people aged 14–22 every year from 1994 onward. Although they took into account factors like education, race, and socioeconomic status, they found that the best predictor of intelligence among all subjects was their mother's IQ.

It's important to note, though, that scientists believe only 40–60 percent of intelligence is hereditary. The environment (school attendance, exposure to books and other learning materials, etc.) still plays a significant factor in one's overall IQ." (MTD Training 2023)

Additional attributes could also be inherited. There are what psychologists call The Big Five, which you may have had the luck, or maybe not, to have at birth.

- The first is an energetic and sociable and friendly disposition, called extroversion.

- The second is moodiness if you have a high level of the trait called neuroticism.

- The third is agreeableness and that includes kindness and affection.

- The fourth is goal orientation which is labeled as conscientiousness. That quality is linked to detail orientation.

- The last is openness. That quality is linked to creativity and adventurousness.

I have given a bit of space to the "organic leader" literature for you to read and ponder. The highfliers who are reading this book can either bask in the glow of your birth or snap your fingers and congratulate yourself for the reading you have done and the colleagues, junior and senior, you have had the luck to work with and learn from. Either way, you can depend on all of the TNTs you study here as stepping stones up the hill of promotion and ever greater leadership roles.

Talking About Highfliers with a Highflier

I am going to go in a slightly different direction for this next interview. As I talked to Jeff Bawol, it became clear to me that *he was the highflier* noticed early by senior people and it paid off. He didn't express it to me that way. It just emerged as he spoke. His is another story about some of the qualities that would lead to being seen as a highflier.

First, a bit about Jeff. He was President of the Americas region at Avnet Technology for nine years but an employee at Avnet for nearly 25 years. He ultimately oversaw 25 supplier lines in the IT distribution channel, was responsible for the Americas strategic direction as well as day-to-day operations. He told me that he started at Hamilton-Avnet Electronics in Detroit, Michigan, after only one year at Wayne State University. I had a feeling in those first few minutes that I would want to use Jeff as the highflier in any discussion about organic leadership.

Jeff began by saying, "I didn't finish college."

> *"I went to Wayne State in Detroit. I had an athletic scholarship and a full ride. After a year I knew it wasn't for me. My siblings were working at Hamilton-Avnet. They sold semiconductors. They hired me. I started in the warehouse counting transistors. Within three months I moved into customer service. After another two months, I moved into a*

sales role. The industry was quickly changing and growing. If you had any ambition, you could move up.

For whatever reason a couple of gentlemen were incredibly generous with their time and attention [and] taught me how to sell. They taught me how to listen and, beyond that, taught me how to be a good person. I learned how to bring a solution to a problem and not bring a problem to a problem. They taught me that if you tell someone you are going to call them back tomorrow at 2PM, you call them back the next day at 2PM whether you have an answer or not. Those nuances of what you do as a salesperson blossomed my career like nobody's business.

I grew in leadership, became a sales manager, a general manager, a regional manager, an area director, and Vice President. I moved over to the computer side of the business, and for whatever reason, another gentleman saw something in me and taught me how to think and not what to think. I learned how to process information. That has been incredibly invaluable to me. He was a great mentor to me. He retired. But the person they hired into that position saw some of the same attributes in me and promoted me to president of that group. He allowed me to make mistakes like nobody's business. We talked in depth about what I had learned and what I would change and how to pass that on to my team.

He asked me, 'If you have an opportunity and it's low risk and high reward, what do you do?' I said, 'We're in.' He asked, 'What if it's medium risk and low reward?' I said, 'We'd move on to the next opportunity.' We spent time talking a lot about risk and reward. I told him that since I was given the right to be wrong, then I would go for the fences. I would go for a home run. If I had a stable business to support a mistake, I would absolutely do that. He sup-ported me and allowed me to progress."

It became clear to me that Jeff's interview was going to be lessons in leadership learned by a highflier as he grew and that I had to share it with you. Here's more:

"This same gentleman had comments about my team. He said they were the most diverse group of people he had ever seen. He asked me how we got along. I told him we challenged each other constantly. We are challenging theses and thought processes and patterns. But whatever we decide on we move on. He said, 'You hire to your weaknesses, not your strengths.' You'll get a diverse group of people that don't all think alike. They don't read the same books. They don't watch the same TV shows. They're different. You get an eclectic group of people who think differently. From that point on I always hired to my weaknesses looking for people smarter than me, and man, that is a hard thing to do. What's the worst thing that can happen? They could become your boss. You hired them so you're probably going to have a good working relationship. How bad can that be? But getting people to do that is really tough. But he taught me to do all those things that I wasn't even aware of doing to be honest with you."

Jeff continued, "I ask myself, if I was a highflier as you say, how did I get here? How did a poor kid from Detroit with no formal edu-cation go from a warehouse job to the president of a 7-billion-dollar company? I always used to say go for the job you want and do that job before you have it. Think about the job you want to have and do that job in addition to the job you have. When your leaders and managers can see you doing that, they will say, 'They are natural. Put them into that job.'"

Jeff wrote the TNTs himself that I want you to study.

- Talk about problems and solutions. "The problem is. The consequences are. The fix is. The benefits are."

- Make commitments and keep them. "I'll have it to you day after tomorrow."

- Offer advice to your peers about critical thinking. I described earlier in the book that critical thinkers might ask, "So what? Who says? Compared to what?"

- Make mistakes and talk about what you learned. "I didn't call them. They decided to go in a different direction. I learned just how a small action, or inaction, can lead to a major disappointment."

- Bring opportunities to your boss and team and show conviction when you say, "Let's swing for the fences." There's a framework I have talked to clients about with the acronym OPEC: Opportunity, Promise, Evidence, Conviction. For instance, "We have a window of opportunity if we act on it. We need to move our facility. If we do, the benefits include faster delivery of our product and a huge revenue upside. We did it two years ago with another warehouse and it proved to be to our advantage. But if we do it we have to be all in and go for the homerun."

Jeff Bawol was a highflier and grew into a career that allowed him to nurture highfliers. Was he born with the qualities he spoke to here or did he develop them as he grew into the job and learned about leadership from observation, from study and maybe from leadership training programs?

There is a TNT I want to give you at this point related to "watching." One of the definitions of genius is "a person who watches what everyone watches but sees what few others see." I have a framework I pass on to my clients called The Scouting Report. You would ask for your boss's attention for a moment and say, "I noticed something in yesterday's meeting [you recount what you saw]. My take on that is [you offer your interpretation of what you saw] and my suggestion to you is…" You would, in essence, be a scout for your boss and/or your team. Your interpretation of what you observed is the chance to show your genius or, let's just say, your highflier skills.

Verbal Skill Builds Trust

I reached out to Allen Meacham because he signed on to a major leadership development program at Boston Scientific Corporation when he was there, and I was one of the facilitators of that effort. It was an audacious and carefully crafted program with a lot of curated presenters. Allen threw his considerable influence to it. Currently, Allen serves as the Chief Revenue Officer at Nalu Medical, Inc. a medical device company in Carlsbad, California, since 2020. He previously held a number of roles at Boston Scientific Corporation including Vice President of U.S. Neuromodulation from 2016 to 2020 and Vice President of Sales from 2008 to 2016. He also worked for Abbott Diagnostics, Bayer Diagnostics, and GlaxoSmithKline in various positions. He received a BS in Business Administration at the University of Arkansas and completed the Advanced Management Program at Harvard Business School.

I asked him, as I asked all my interviewees, to tell me about a highflier that drew his attention.

"One of the things that jumped out at me was their verbal communication skills. It's just a fact. You see it and you

are like, wow. The one I am thinking about showed up, maybe in a small meeting or on a stage. There was some quality there that was so compelling. That kind of thing gets a lot of credit and maybe it can be overvalued but there it is … verbal communication skill. It just drew me in. It made me want to trust them, follow them, and respond to them. That was the first thing. And maybe my personality has something to do with it. That quality is something I have always responded to. Then he showed up and was great at the job. But the verbal communication skill is what I noticed first."

Allen also offered some advice about things a highflier should *not* do.

"A person came to us with a great resume. They had a big personality and looked the part in every way. They turned out to be one of the most annoying people in the entire organization. They would come by my office on a regular basis asking for feedback. I finally said, 'Look, I'm not giving you any more feedback because you haven't done any of the things I've suggested you do. You ask for feedback but continue to be the same person. I would never try to change everything about you but there have been a few things you needed to attend to. You have had a 360. You need to put all that together.' Instead of looking for ways to help them develop as a highflier, I was looking for ways to get away from them."

Allen's comment took me back to the first book I wrote, *So Smart But…: How Intelligent People Lose Credibility—and How They Can Get it Back*. It is all about people described as, in some cases, brilliant but having problematic communication issues. There have been a few instances when I have been asked to work with someone on, let's say, better board presentations. After a meeting or two, their boss would ask, "How did it go?" My client would say, "Oh … just alright. I've heard it all before." That is not a good idea. If you are given a plan for improving something and a resource to help, do not make the gift seem like a bad investment.

The TNT about responding to feedback is (1) do your best, of course, to improve on the issues you asked about, or (2) at minimum, talk about what you are doing to try and address it.

But back to the highflier Allen Meacham told me about.

> *"I could go to them and say, 'I need to have a tough conversation with you.' They were taken aback of course. Everyone is taken a little aback sometimes. But then they said, 'I am going to figure this out. I'll come back and check in with you. I have a game plan for it. I want to be held accountable for it.' They forced me, in a way, to be a mentor. I thought if they were willing to engage with me, I would take them up on it. I admire the people who will give the feedback and remain engaged, and I really admire those that take the feedback and run with it."*

Finally, Allen said:

> *"There was a person who was an engineer by training. They had gotten into the quality part of the organization and had worked their way into a field job working with patients. I saw something in them right away. It started with everything we talked about. They carried themselves with a real physical presence. They had a warm smile. I began coaching them to take credit for being an engineer.*

I said, 'Stand up and tell them what degree you have and why you deserve to be in front of them.' They took that advice and started doing it. Then they came to work for me in a sales training job. Then they asked to go back to the field. Then they asked to come back in. It was back and forth. I came across a PowerPoint the other day that they had put together. They had included all the things that they needed to do. We put a plan together and did it. Today they have a directorship at their company and have 50 people reporting to them."

The tip for "taking credit" means repeating this to yourself: *I love what I do and they need to hear it.*

The Obvious Desire to Gain Broad Understanding Through Question Asking

I worked with MaryAnn Miller when she was at Avent in Phoenix in 2020. MaryAnn received Arizona State University's W.P. Carey School of Business Distinguished Achievement Award in 2010. She holds a bachelor's degree in Political Science from the University of Illinois and a master's in Business Administration from Arizona State University, W.P. Carey School of Business. She was a terrific supporter of "added preservatives" in that she offered employees a variety of programs to enhance their leadership skills, born or not.

Here's how she began talking about a highflier.

"I first heard this highflier talking in a meeting with such a broad perspective on the issue for her time and role. Part of it was the way she asked questions to gain even a broader understanding, and it was generally questions about things that were not obvious and that is something

that less talented people often do … ask about the obvious. So often they ask about things that are right in front of them. I think of it as asking questions 'from the side.' They asked, 'What is this and what is that?' because those are the questions that impact what is right in front of them. It is such a pleasure when I say to myself after interesting questions are asked, 'Hmmm. I had not thought about that.'

This person had the bigger picture right from the start. This person and I became friends. She was in their mid-30s. Her capacity for understanding things was way beyond her years and was on the level of someone who had many more years of experience. She was always determined to learn and grow.

My first impressions came at an interview. She took over a department where she already had been working. I wanted to learn more about her, so I spent more time talking about various issues. I would ask, 'What are your thoughts on what is going on there in your function? Are we on track? What are we missing?' The level of thinking was so much bigger than expected for her time in the position. And speaking of natural born leadership, and that is sometimes a perception I would have, other members of the group had a huge level of respect for her. Of course I nurtured it by encouraging her.

I was also impressed with the way she carried herself. There was a way of walking with seemingly a purpose to where she was going in the building. It would have been hard to ignore. And when she talked about the work, she was never trying to impress me. She certainly never talked about why she should be the leader. She simply offered information with facts and data along with where she thought all of that might be leading to support our vision. She was just on a different plane than most people.

Now having said all that, some of her peers did not see her as humble. Some of it might have been cultural. Her natural tone was authoritative. But no one most certainly questioned her capability. She was somewhat demanding, and I liked that. I am somewhat like that myself and so I appreciate it in others. She was given the feedback and responded to it by, again, asking questions and had no issues addressing it. She did things, like reading and working with a coach that offered tangible ways to show she was responding to it.

As to communication style, in presentations she sometimes talked too much. Her slides had too much stuff on them. A slide might not get to the meat of the message. But she was to the point when we had one-on-one conversations. In those settings, I was excited about her analysis of things. She had an extensive, deep knowledge of the digital world. I had not come from that, but I had ideas that she could help blossom. Those talks created a spark and solidified the vision she had.

One thing I would recommend to all potential highfliers is to recount what had happened with this or that customer. I would be asking about her thoughts on customers and suppliers and their reaction to our products and she could always describe their comments to me. She said, 'This customer said such and such.' And she was excited about it as she talked. I also appreciated her level of enthusiasm as expressed through her voice and mannerisms. She knew where our suppliers' gaps were and how what we had could be valuable for them.

So, her thoughts did not just reflect her coming up with brilliant ideas but came from input from others. And what she said helped me as I then sold an idea up the organization. As much as we talk about leadership, we cannot ignore a highflier's taking the role of excellent staff work. Selling ideas to my leadership was a big deal, change was a big deal. Digital could be a threat to our traditional model. Everything had to be cushioned and presented in a thoughtful way. They would want to know how something would complement our existing model and what another avenue for sales could be."

MaryAnn had one last comment but it certainly was not the least: "I would go to a conference that customers attended. This highflier would give me things to talk to them about. I loved that she was pro-active. I did not have the subject matter expertise. But that highflier knew what she was trying to accomplish and could speak the lingo. This person would give me topics to initiate a conversation." This is simply another example of excellent staff work.

The TNTs growing out of MaryAnn's interview are coming right at you. I am going to start at the top:

- Questions that are "not obvious" often start with "why" and "how" and "what." Those have traditionally been called open ended. But that doesn't mean it ends there. Start with one of those and then follow up with questions seeking a "yes" or "no." A "right in front of you" question would be "How long have they been doing this?" You would be expected to know that. But "how does it compare to the other options?" is from the side. That could be followed up with "Do we have the capacity to do even more?" MaryAnn asked these questions.

167

Keep your ears open for the questions asked by your boss. She said that she would ask, "What are your thoughts on what is going on there in your function? Are we on track? What are we missing?"

- Walk as if you are going to a specific place, maybe a meeting down the hall. People who have been in the military bring that quality to work and it is noticed.

- Minimize the explanations that start with "I." It isn't as if you have to say "we." Neither pronoun has to be there. Have a bias toward words like this: "The idea seemed to take hold. The reactions were thoughtful. Their suggestions were helpful."

- As has come up before, minimize the amount of content on a slide. That seems to always imply a tactical mindset and not a strategic one. If there is a lot on a slide, use words to start it like, "The point that was intended here is _____. Take a look at this ..."

- "Somewhat demanding" implies a lack of sufficient polite words. If your intention is to say, "Make sure I have it by 3PM," your demand is softer if you say, "Do your best to have it to me by 3PM." As is often said, "words matter."

- Before you lead, be the best support person you can be. Think of yourself as a paid consultant to the person you report to. Help them be the best leader they can be. My practice thrived because I did not call myself an "executive coach"... EVER. I always described myself as my client's senior support person for communication and credibility issues.

Chapter 10

Influence Skills Absolutely Necessary

I watched as they changed the minds of ten people.

If I were a chef, influence skills would be my signature dish. Le Cordon Bleu, in my case, was the Master's Program at West Virginia University where my research program began. Just like a chef would swoon at seeing a basket of black truffles, I had a similar reaction the first time I saw a book chapter headed "Persuasion: Approach to Gaining Compliance." In this case, the book was *Human Communication* by Michael Burgoon and Michael Ruffner. I have referenced it earlier in this book but not in relation to persuasion and influence.

Communication training is, if you look at it globally, about informing or persuading. Informing itself has a persuasive quality to it. Informing, like a college lecture, does not stand on its own. Anyone who has taught can tell you that the first questions asked in a lecture usually start with, "Yes, but what about this other thing?" Students are not always confident that what they are hearing in an otherwise informative lecture is the unvarnished truth. Given the need to be talented when it comes to attitude change, this chapter's intention is to give the techniques to you. It is absolutely necessary for a highflier.

Some Research on Influence Skills

I want to start the research part of this chapter with this from *Human Communication*:

> *"An unwillingness to be persuaded is not an isolated phenomenon in the communication process. Any of the same personal factors that obstruct other forms of communication similarly shape our resistance to the overt or implicit influence of others. As we mature, certain of our ideas about the nature of reality tend toward becoming absolute convictions; our affective behavior follows more or less fixed patterns; and our cognitive processes—that is the way in which we think, analyze, and interpret—become less open to change. Communicators who seek to influence our attitudes, emotions, and perceptual framework often must deal with rather ingrained tendencies and predispositions.*
>
> *The tenacity of our past ways of thinking, feeling, and perceiving probably accounts for the fact that persuasive communication sometimes fails to be effective even when most logically and directly planned and most heavily substantiated by reasons for change.*
>
> *Why, how, and in what ways people are persuaded to change—anything from their brand of toothpaste to their political party—is the interesting subject of several communication theories."*

Before I review a few of those theories, I want to give you some insight into how our minds grapple with ideas.

A Variety of Ways to Measure Attitudes on a Variety of Topics

Our ideas are "floating," you could say, on a continuum between two distinct poles on every topic. It is generally not a simple love-hate bipolar choice. Try to picture a survey you have filled out to rate a product. Every commercial entity now sends a post-experience survey for you to complete that they hope to make available to other potential customers. The survey producers deploy what is called a *semantic-differential scale* for you to express your attitude. Your attitude is expressed by opposite adjectives at each end of the scale. It might be satisfied-unsatisfied, would recommend to others or would not recommend to others, and various points in between. Charles Osgood, an American psychologist, created the scale so that attitudes toward a topic could be recorded and researched.

Here's an example if you were asked about an experience at a doctor's office. You could slide along the line until it reflected your opinion.

Very Pleasant	Somewhat Pleasant	Neither Pleasant nor Unpleasant	Somewhat Unpleasant	Very Unpleasant

Another type of scale to measure attitude is called the *Likert Scale*. It asks those who complete the survey to show their agreement or disagreement with a statement. It looks like this.

Strongly Disagree	Disagree	Moderately Disagree	Neutral	Moderately Agree	Agree	Strongly Agree

Suppose you asked your team members to complete the Likert Scale before pitching an idea at a meeting. The topic might be "Offering this product would be a good move." Each of six team members would complete the scale. If four of the six indicated "strongly disagree," you would have the task of trying to get them to move their attitude *toward* the right side, the "strongly agree" side, after your presentation was done. And here's the thing: You should not begin by thinking you have to move them all the way to "strongly agree." Your task is to move them toward it. That movement, and the subsequent conversations you have with them that move them along, is truly how "influence skills" are tested. And some are better at that than others. That is what this chapter is about.

Here is how I have always described the movement of attitude along the scale. If you imagine a person's attitude was shown by an "x" at a certain spot on the scale, your job is to get that "x" to move in the direction you want. Think of it as firmly rooted on the line. That is certainly possible given that most of us have entrenched opinions on various issues. That "x" needs "lift" to get it moving. Your message, if it is done properly, gives that "x" lift. Think of a helicopter lifting from the helipad before moving toward its destination. Once you get lift, there's a chance to move it in the right direction, your stated direction. I am going to describe here the qualities that give their attitude "lift."

Suppose you worked in marketing for a theme park. You were following statistics measuring visits over the past three years. You are concerned about the drop in repeat visits from the same customers. You have been given the task of convincing management to lower the price of a day ticket. The majority of your listeners in management want the price to stay the same or even increase, believing that inflation is a real issue and that the park is so popular, people will adjust to the increase in price.

You start your presentation by saying, "The cost of being at the park is going up while the perks are going away. We interviewed one gentleman who said, 'The cost of a one-day ticket for myself and my wife along with a one-night stay at the on-site hotel was $900. The same trip three years ago was $550. It's hard to justify coming to the park when we could probably go on a cruise for the same money.'" Your hope is that the quote was compelling enough for some members of the audience to move their "x" from "Strongly Disagree" with lowering the price to "Disagree" or even "Moderately Disagree." That would be good enough to start the ball rolling toward a management decision to offer discounts. And that is an example of why the job this presenter took came with the job description "Influence Skills Absolutely Necessary."

Weaving Together Words That Persuade

Now that you've learned about scales; some research. Dolores Albarracin and Sharon Shavitt published an excellent review of attitude change studies in 2017.

> *"The study of attitudes is the study of evaluations, and it has been a part of social psychology since that field first emerged with Thomas & Znaniecki's (1918–1920) The Polish Peasant in Europe and America. The term attitude was initially used by Jung (1923) in his writing about psychological types to describe a readiness to respond, a definition later incorporated by Allport (1935). However, as there are no guarantees that, for example, liking a political candidate will yield support for that candidate at the polls, overt behavioral responses are no longer part of the definition of attitudes."*
>
> *—(Albarracin and Shavitt 2017)*

The authors go on to explain that we can ask people to tell us what their attitude is or infer it from their reactions to hearing or reading something: "A search for research on attitudes in the *Journal of Personality and Social Psychology* ... shows ongoing interest.... A count of articles whose abstracts mention attitude, persuasion, belief, opinion, or evaluative judgments reveals that such articles comprise a fairly steady 20% of publications."

The research foci are wide ranging. Just to take one example, a linguistic technique I have been interested in since my early days studying communication is metaphor. I always wondered if people who are talented with figurative language like metaphor and simile and analogy are more likely to succeed in their efforts to change attitudes in an audience than those who are not so inclined. Albarracin and Shavitt wrote, "The use of metaphors and their impact on attitudes is one important focus of investigation. For instance, reading about the police as either guardians or warriors led to, respectively, more and less liking for the police." (Thibodeau et al. 2017)

TNT: You need to compare your idea or product to something found in nature. For instance, "Our distribution system is like honeybees distributing pollen. It's as smooth and efficient as those bees."

People Skilled at Manipulating Others Possess Unique Language Skills

My own empirical research on attitude change included a study I conducted for my Master's Thesis: "Machiavellianism (Mach) is a personality variable that has been shown to exist in persons who formulate strategies for manipulating others (Christie 1968) in communication activities particularly in bargaining situations (Hurt 1972). A high Machiavellian is seen as more capable of 'winning' in bargaining situations with low Machs when the situation provides for: (1) face to face interaction with other participants; (2) when the interaction is relatively unstructured; and (3) when there is a high degree of 'irrelevant affect' (reacting to the speaker rather than the content of the message) in the event (Christie 1970). The small group environment provides for these kinds of situations and various investigators have used a small group in their research." (Weiner 1973)

Personality, language choice, clarity in speaking and writing, energy level, and so on have all been studied to try to understand the persuasion and influence process.

TNT: Machiavellians ask others to argue your position in the group setting. It would sound like this: "Jack, just to be sure you understand my view on this, could you say it so I can agree that you do, in fact, understand me?" Stating a viewpoint counter to that of Jack's attitude often moves Jack closer to your position.

Power and Authenticity

I want to report on another research focus because of the type of client I have and the audiences they try to influence. The conclusion of one study is that "high-power communicators generate messages with greater competence information, and high-power audiences are persuaded more by competence information … low-power communicators generate messages with greater warmth information, and low-power audiences are persuaded more by warmth information." (Dubois, Rucker, and Galinsky 2016)

TNT: To translate that, the quality of highflier my interviewees talk about and the audiences they speak to are, no doubt, high-power. That means messages that are logically organized and supported with data are going to be more influential on the senior level audience than messages relying on emotion. What does emotion imply?

- More voice volume and modulation.
- Lively facial expression over low affect.

- Posture and active gestures.

- Figurative language with more analogy and metaphor.

All those qualities are generally appreciated. But the research would suggest that disciplined, organized, and data-driven content wins out with a senior level audience.

There are also thought-provoking research findings about an influencer's receivers. In fact, this is a good time to summarize all communication research as springing from four categories. An acronym to remember is SMCR: Source, message, channel, and receiver.

- There are studies about the impact of the speaker or the source of the message.

- Of course, there is so much research about the quality of the message. You have read here about word choice, sentence length, and organizing principle such as problem, cause, consequence, and solution.

- Another category of study centers on the channel the message is sent through. In our time, the time of writing this book, you may be talking to people face to face, on a conference call with only voices, and on a conference call that is virtual, as well as the impact of your written documents and emails. That's what is meant by "channel."

- Finally, research about who you are communicating with. That is referred to as the receivers.

When it comes to receivers and how to tailor your message to them, I have been asked more times than I remember to deliver a speech or seminar on message and style variations for Boomers, Gen X, Millennials, and Gen Z. The question is always, "How can we tailor our messages to different generations of listeners?" That is another book.

The issue I have been asked to address when generational differences come up in conversation, more than any other, is authenticity. To be an influencer, you must appear authentic to your listeners. They are less tolerant of artifice than older listeners have historically been. When my son, a Millennial, tells me, a Baby Boomer, that so and so is a "hypocrite" I patiently said, "What's new? That is what politics requires of candidates so they can appeal to a variety of voter values and attitudes." He yearns for authentic candidates.

My major TNT about authenticity as a quality I would want every highflier to show is consistency in attitude from day to day, week to week, and month to month as the topics you are responsible for continue to be discussed. That is what is meant by "keepin' it real."

The Risks of Complex Words Related to Sounding Like a "Consultant Type"

Here's an interview that puts honesty and authenticity at the forefront of a highflier's ability to persuade. Amie Krause joined Revance in March 2023 as Chief People Officer, overseeing human resources and people functions, including culture initiatives, employee relations, total rewards, diversity and inclusion, leadership development, talent acquisition, as well as corporate affairs.

Amie has more than 25 years of experience in the biotech industry as a senior human resources leader. Prior to joining Revance, she was the SVP and Chief People Officer at Atara Biotherapeutics in Thousand Oaks, California, where she led people strategies, company growth, culture, and employee development. Prior to Atara, Amie worked for Amgen in a number of human resources roles of increasing responsibility, including her role as Global HR Lead, Organizational Effectiveness during which she served as the Human Resources Leader for Amgen's global commercial operations covering the Americas, Europe, Asia, and the Middle East. Prior to

Amgen, Amie held multiple Talent Acquisition roles in the services and gaming industries.

Here is Amie's highflier. This is a story about simple wording that left an honest and authentic impression.

> *"I remember a presentation. When I first interacted with him, he would have been in his late 20s. I saw a presentation or maybe a section of a presentation. What struck me was a level of honesty that I really appreciated. I think so many people try to come off as a consultant type. You know, the kind from one of the top consulting firms. I don't have to mention a name. They are so smart and use big words and try to overly impress. But this highflier had a level of humility. If he did not know the answer to a question, he would not try to fake it or paper over it with words. He was very straightforward with simple language. It gave him a level of honesty that I thought came across as somebody who was confident in who they were. He knew the subject matter. He was a subject matter expert with a command of it. He realized he did not have to overtly impress. Honest, straightforward, and with humility. There was no need to have a conversation filled with meaningless words. He was direct, fast, and honest. And that made this person a terrific influencer."*

Here come some tips and tools:

- Repeat: Use one-syllable English. It sounds "real" and real is very close to honesty. If you intend to say, "We implemented a process that should please all the stakeholders," I encourage you to instead say, "We've put a process in place that everyone involved will like."

- When you don't know the answer to a question, say, "I don't have the precise number. I *can* tell you it is much higher than we expected."

Somebody I trust is going to help me let my guard down and be influenced … kind of automatically. It's like, "I trust what you are telling me, and now I am going to invite you in to be able to influence me." There you have it. Communication ability, the root of which is simple words that create the bud of honesty and authenticity and blossoms into persuasion and influence. How's that for another metaphor?

Successful Influence Requires Storytelling

Continuing my determination to give my readers, my fliers hoping to be highfliers, the best possible advice, I interviewed Caroline Stokell. Caroline is the CEO of Meridiem Investment in London. She has managed global equity portfolios and relationships for international clients and charities for more than 20 years. Her experience as board director and trustee brings a wealth of knowledge and understanding of management, culture, and corporate governance to the investment team.

Her investment career began in 2000 at Newton Investment Management, where she went on to join the Board of Newton's Jersey business and to head up their International Private Clients' team. Caroline was Newton's designated senior manager for anti-money laundering and financial crime (2010–2012), a responsibility she also held at Meridiem.

She holds an MA (Hons) from the University of St. Andrews and is an Associate of the Chartered Institute for Securities and Investment.

Here is Caroline's thinking on what we hope to see in junior people striving to succeed.

"*There are people that hook us to thinking they are our collective potential for the future. I am personally observing the enduring nature of communication, really good communication, in the way people tell stories. No matter what the medium is because there are so many more places that you must communicate or receive information from. There are people who can shift the wheat from the chaff and that is an important signal. What gets said and how is it said?*

Several people come to my mind on this topic. The first thing I spotted was optimism. They make you want to harness their energy and connect with them. You want to nurture their ideas and help them work through their ideas. Do you remember Eeyore and Tigger? No one follows Eeyore. They always follow Tigger. Eeyore is negative and Tigger is optimistic. And Tigger is full of energy too. That makes them so much more influential and able to sway attitudes toward solutions ... helpful solutions. That is one of the things that really stands out for me. Of course they don't always have the right answers. But their willingness to explore things in a positive and constructive, solution oriented way is necessary to persuade others in a group setting.

There is another person I am thinking of who was a trainee. They are now a portfolio manager and moving into a leadership position. They will have their first direct report this year. When you start to expand beyond doing your day job and begin doing the people job, it takes the ability to influence others, getting them to do things, managing the people on the side as well. And that can be quite distracting. They have more on their plate. Things can fall off the plate. It also takes humility to accept that when a mistake has been made, the good ones learn to accept it. They may have gotten things wrong. But they have developed a preparedness to fail. It is a real sign that if you are prepared to be wrong you won't get crushed. Otherwise, it just gets harder. The demands are bigger. The leadership expectations increase. Failures can be more costly and publicly more difficult than when you are junior.

Being able to spot in someone, as I have in the person I am thinking about, is a fortunate find because they are better able to handle things. In one example, they thought they made a big dealing error, quite big as a matter of fact, that would cost 50,000 pounds to correct. But they had a willingness to be wrong. They went to the client and, due to great influence skills, said, 'I've made a mistake.' In actual fact, a mistake had not been made at all. This willingness to course-correct, to start again is so impressive. The benefit to the firm is the degree to which other team members see this and are influenced by the model it provides."

I asked Caroline if there were qualities in the "next generation" that are particularly impressive.

"There are things in the next generation that show abilities better than I had at the same starting point. The things I see in the younger ones make me wish I had done the same things at their age. One of them would have made me much more able to influence others. It starts, of course, with listening before they communicate. They are prepared to do the drudgery for preparation. But when they start talking, they back things up with facts and anecdotes. They demonstrate the adage that less is more when they have to get others to come along with their ideas. If I ask for more data, they have it to offer. They have all this substance behind them. They do not start reversing up a truck and

dumping a load of information and data that my crazy brain has to start sifting through as they present. They can influence us to buy and sell stock. They can move the dial. They influence us because their message is organized and they are open to listening and to collaborate with all of us on the team. To collaborate with them is magic. I could talk for hours about this.

Before I forget, one of my pet peeves is talking over people. The highflier in my mind never does that. When a person has a lot of energy, they can unintentionally not let someone else finish a thought before jumping in. Great listeners do not do that. It drives me mad. It's obvious when that happens that you are just waiting to speak but have a hard time waiting. That is a sign that someone is not going to be a great leader. Great leaders speak less, say less and listen more."

What TNTs can you gather from Caroline?

- One tip on storytelling is, when the opening words are "About a week (or whatever) ago," the listener knows immediately a story is coming. It makes for very easy listening. Without effort, your word choice will come naturally.

- Predict a good outcome if things are done right as opposed to a negative outcome if things are not done right.

- Keep doing what you've always done when things were going well. I don't want others to stop at your desk and say, "What's wrong? Are you okay?"

- One of my professors once said to me in front of the whole class, "Weiner, I am much more coherent in full sentences." That was all it took.

Know What You're Talking About, and Be Poised While Talking About It

I've had good fortune in knowing and working with the experts I have introduced you to throughout this book. I had the pleasure of interviewing Joe Newell. Joe is the CEO of Sastra Cell Therapy in Southern California. Joe previously worked as the Chief Operations Officer at Atara Biotherapeutics from March 2020 to March 2022. In this role, Joe was responsible for defining a comprehensive global manufacturing plan, long-term global supply chain, building an engineering services capability, establishing a comprehensive logistics and distribution capability, and ultimately positioning Atara for years to come to ensure patients have availability to Atara's therapies no matter where they live.

From April 2017 to March 2020, Joe Newell served as the Executive Vice President, Technical Operations at Atara Biotherapeutics. Prior to Atara Biotherapeutics, Joe was with Alexion Pharmaceuticals, Inc. from June 2015 to March 2017 as the Vice President, North America Manufacturing. In this role, Joe was responsible for leading Alexion's North American Manufacturing organization and overseeing all aspects of commercial product supply for Alexion's products manufactured in the United States and Puerto Rico. He completed his undergraduate degree at California State Polytechnic University-Pomona with a BS in Biology. Joe then attended Loyola Jesuit College Preparatory for a post-secondary education degree.

Joe told me this about highfliers:

> *"On the topic of highfliers, I've given this a lot of thought. The person I've chosen had qualities that I knew early on were special. First, they knew what they were talking about. You could tell they had done their homework and were poised talking about it. And speaking of influence skills, they had*

the attention of my peers and supervisors. I was impressed with what I saw, especially in a big corporation, where everyone feels they need to be proven right and part of the solution. I was impressed with their attitude of acknowledging positions taken by someone else and then adding value to them. It was often, 'Yeah that's a great perspective and we are looking at that.' And there was an openness to ideas that they had not thought of without being defensive. That is a rare quality and one of the things that made them so able to influence others in the meeting.

There was a positive energy and it was an authentic energy. It wasn't political. It wasn't salesmanship. It was an authentic energy around the topic and the interest in getting that topic or problem associated with it resolved. And lastly, there was an attitude of pleasantness about problem solving. They were excited without being too excited. You had the feeling of 'Hey, I'm around the big shots but I'm comfortable in my own shoes.' It's the potential for solving the problem that created the excitement and not just being around big shots.

They were a director at the time but now are a Senior Vice President and I'm sure are getting groomed for something much, much bigger. There was a poise under fire that has contributed so much to their success. When I say 'under fire,' folks are peppering you with objections to the facts you present or the potential solution. But that authentic energy to help the company was effective. They read the room so well and could do it quickly. It was like, 'This is why I'm here and this is the issue I am going after. Here are the facts and the data.' That is why they were thought of as a great storyteller.

On top of that, they were efficient with time and communication style. They gave only the facts that were necessary for listeners to understand and kept at the right level for the engagement. They had very important topics to cover. And they also were good at teeing things up. Problems were solved and done according to plan. There was an ability to tee up with realism of what needed to be done. Then they went out and got it done.

I want to add that they made sure the room wasn't too big for them. There might have been vice presidents and senior vice presidents. These meetings were what you could call pretty big meetings in that sense with big problems to solve. It never seemed, with this highflier, that the room had become too big. It was a nice job of assimilating to the humans in the room and not the titles in the room. This person knew what was in it for each of them. Some people were active stakeholders in solving the problem. Some people were bystanders. There were support people. It was as if they choreographed the orchestra. There would be a dozen or more people in the meeting in different layers above them. But they were prepared. I really respected the preparation and the knowledgeable aura resulting from that. There was also the authenticity of acknowledging what they knew and did not know, taking feedback from the audience in such a way that they never, ever turned their attention to someone else. Never."

And now the TNTs:

- "You could tell they had done their homework and were poised talking about it."

  Influence depends on crisp, simply spoken descriptions with minimum hesitations, plenty of eye contact to show courage and minimum body movement.

- "I was impressed with their attitude of acknowledging positions taken by someone else and then adding value to them."

  Try saying something as simple as "You're spot on and I have a good example of that."

- "And there was an openness to ideas that they had not thought of without being defensive."

  A good statement to make: "I missed that, and it makes so much sense as I hear you describe it."

- "You had the feeling of 'Hey, I'm around the big shots but I'm comfortable in my own shoes.'"

  Speaking in plain words, not consultant-speak, accounts for this compliment.

- "When I say 'under fire,' folks are peppering you with objections to the facts you present or the potential solution."

  Objections are made, not with questions but with statements. They often start with "It seems to me that..." Turn the statement into a question and then answer it. I encourage you to say, "If you are asking me about _____, my take on that would be _____."

- "And they also were good at teeing things up."

  Start this way: "Four weeks ago we were asked to look at _____. One of the questions specifically was _____. Today we're here to give you our plan."

- "There was also the authenticity of acknowledging what they knew and did not know, taking feedback from the audience in such a way that they never, ever turned their attention to someone else."

I encourage you to say, in answer to questions that you can't answer in the moment, "I don't have that number. I'll get it for you. But one thing I DO know is…"

In this book, there may be TNTs I have suggested more than once. The beauty of them is the potential for one skill to have many benefits. There will be many times when people will say, "I don't know exactly what they do that creates such a terrific impression, but whatever it is, I can only say they are a highflier and I hope we continue to attract more of them."

Chapter 11

For All Generations: Making Your Mark and Being a Mentor

In the wake of the interviews you have read all through this book, and knowing I had even more to conduct, I decided to fill your minds with a variety of qualities that my guest interviewees cited as special to highfliers without topical guardrails. We don't need research on each interview. I am going to let them stand on their own. They not only have thoughts on highfliers. They have insights about the contributions you make to your team, your company, and most importantly, yourselves.

I experienced a lift, an exhilarating uplift of joy, after ending each Zoom call with my interviewees. It's been a gift to spend several weeks talking with some inspiring men and women in business and industry, law, and academia. If this opportunity had been a course I enrolled in at Harvard or Cambridge, a course offering a chance to listen to these people, those schools would be justified in charging me hundreds of thousands of dollars.

A Passion, an Obsession, to Help Humanity

I pray I have laid these interviews out in a way that allows you to soak up these lessons. My interviewees were so generous with their time because this particular issue, the secret of, as André Hoelz said, discovering people who "can light up a dark stage," is just as fascinating to them as it has been to me.

I am going to begin with André. He is the Mary and Charles Ferkel Professor of Chemistry and Biochemistry at California Institute of Technology in Pasadena, California. He received a Bachelor of Science degree from Albert-Ludwigs University of Freiburg in 1993, a Master of Science degree from Albert-Ludwigs in 1997, his PhD from Rockefeller University in 2004, and has been on the faculty at Caltech since 2010. He was named Howard Hughes Medical Institute Investigator in 2024.

First, I will lay out an outline of André's lengthy interview topics and then open them up with more detail. It will become ever clearer to you as you read why I decided to reserve this chapter for a brainstorming session on highfliers. Here are the topics André spoke to:

- Curiosity
- The role of passion and effort
- Mentorship and environment
- Risk taking and fearlessness
- Impact over perfectionism
- Natural ability vs. learned skills
- Enthusiasm and communication
- Making a difference for us all

André began with curiosity.

"Yes, here at Caltech this happens regularly. You find a person, a series of people, that you think will do something incredible. Yes, they are different. When they move on, they have done incredible things. They have, there is, something in common about them. I have seen a series of properties. At the end it's curiosity. You have

a conversation with them and their eyes light up. You tell them about something and a passion is ignited with intrinsic curiosity and a serious drive to make an impact, followed by a spark to stick with it … it won't be deterred. Yes, there's intelligence. At Caltech and at Rockefeller this was a common thing. They have a developed craft. They know math. But ultimately there is that curiosity and the unbelievable amount of drive to bring, in the end, real impact.

I will give you an example. There was an undergraduate who worked with me. Then he did his master's thesis, with me again, then did the PhD somewhere else. Every single time there was a new encounter, you could see he made an unbelievable jump. He came back for a post-doc. This person was a 'tank' that could work 20 hours a day nonstop. He felt he needed to do this to get the work done, every day, nonstop for a year. This person is now senior vice president of a financial company. He is no longer in experimental science. But he brought the same skill set to the new job. Now he assesses other people's scientific qualities as well as the qualities of companies. So, very smart, very inquisitive, very motivated. At the end, they just 'blow through' obstacles.

One thing these people must watch out for is they can get bored. They are very smart and want to do something, but they can get bored. They can get deterred. They cannot handle the boredom of the routine because 95 percent of the work is repetition and trying to make things better. There is a degree of perfectionism there. Once they intellectually figure things out, they can lose interest and the work to bring their ideas home falls to others. But the good ones do not get bored."

André then talked about passion and perfectionism.

"I had an undergraduate who came to me in her first year. She did not know anything about research but had tremendous enthusiasm. At the end of the undergrad program, she applied for a PhD position that would not be generic. These folks are different than the average, let's say. They make strategic choices where they think things about something very deep like science itself. 'What will this, if I invest in it, do to give me my strength where I strengthen my skill set?' They ask themselves, 'How can I maximize this?' In this case, she was one of the best students I ever had and made a big splash. She was interested in how the body senses things on a molecular level. It's a difficult thing to identify talent like that. There are just so many strengths that a person has to have. But at the end, if they have a passion and a degree of perfectionism, they are ones that will stick it out … for themselves and for an impact to humanity.

It's so much a matter of investing time. It's like a piano player. How much must one practice to make themselves better? And then the technical thing gets done. You are starting to play in a way that connects with the music. And one other thing: This is such a competitive business that if you do not really have a passion for it, it will be unbelievably painful to fake it. The people around you, they will have this trait and at the end of the day will say, 'Well, you go to the beach. I want to go to the lab.'"

André also talked about mentorship.

"I also need to say something about accepting feedback and integrating it in a non-confrontational way. I would

say to somebody, 'This is awesome. This is how I would do it.' One should learn from this and learn from other people how they would do it and it will be better, and it will improve you as a person. A person I have in my mind right now sucks feedback up like a sponge. You see them the next time and they have incorporated all of your feedback into their work. And you know what? They make an unbelievable jump. A non-pretentious person, and believe me there are good reasons to be a bit pretentious here at Caltech, basically allows themselves to readily learn from others. That is a capital M Major asset in getting ahead. From the five- or six-year PhD to a five-year post-doc, to being a faculty member, you are constantly improving. To learn from others is so important in what we do. If one does not have this, at the end it holds a lot of great students back—great people back actually. They just cannot have the attitude of 'Well, I am already great.'"

A few final words from André:

"There is an inherent bias to look for someone exactly like you. I was not the smartest of all the people around me. But I had a will to make something happen. And you can find these people and can tell very fast, in a conversation sometimes, whether somebody has a passion for something. It's in small moments. If I asked this person, for instance, 'Tell me what you have done today' and they start talking. And then I say, 'You solved the structure of something and the molecule. So tell me what it looks like.' And they say, 'Oh my God, there's this thing here. And that thing there. It is so cool.' That is the moment when the magic happens because you cannot fake this. You cannot fake that kind of enthusiasm.

There is something that one of my colleagues, Peter Dervan, used to say about people who stick out. 'The lights go on, on a stage in total darkness.' That is so much fun. You want to be a part of their education. The highflier I am thinking about all through this interview is someone to whom I said, 'You're going to blow everyone out of the water.' She said, 'I want to learn as much as possible.'

Here are a few TNTs from André's interview:

- Ask "Why does this matter?"
- Ask "How does this compare to alternatives?"
- Do your level best to feel passion and to show it.
- Don't wait for feedback. Ask for it.

"I Love Your Idea"

With more than 20 years of experience, Ross Ciesla joined Veritas in 2010. It is now a part of Meridiem. Previously, Ross was a Director of Investment Management at Newton Investment Management, where he was the lead fund manager for segregated, balanced pension schemes, in addition to managing portfolios on behalf of charities and private individuals. Ross completed his postgraduate studies at Johns Hopkins University and holds an MA in Economics from Aberdeen University. He is a Member of the Chartered Institute for Securities and Investment.

Here is how Ross first encountered the highflier that came to his mind.

"One of the things that stuck out to me about this person was something they did not do as opposed to something they

did. They were a part of a meeting where a lot of people were contributing their ideas. I have a pet peeve about the way people add on to what someone else said. It annoys me when people jump in just as soon as someone else finishes with words like, 'It's not just that, it's also ...(my point).' Often, with young analysts someone will say something good, and rather than giving them space so that someone else can say, 'That's great,' they throw in, 'It's not just that. It's also this really interesting point over here.' That is not supportive. And supportive is one of my most sought-after traits in a team member. I know what that does to the person who has said what they've said with their hearts thumping in front of a big group. They hope someone will say, 'well done.' It goes back to the mentorship thing with each of them helping each other on the journey they are on."

Ross is offering some ideas here that certainly qualify as coming from a mentor who wants you to succeed!

"The example I just gave you, Allen, is playground stuff. It's the playground, but we see it in companies. My highflier does not do that. I sometimes say that team competition is good, but I do not like seeing a hugely cutthroat competition in the office. I have compared this to the Beatles. They were really competitive. Paul McCartney would write 'Penny Lane,' and Lennon would say, 'Oh, that's such a good idea. I'll see if I can build on that.' Then Lennon would come out with 'Strawberry Fields.' That's the competition I like to see, and my highflier had it and still has it. They say, 'I love your idea. I'm going to tweak what I am doing and use your structure.' In that way you end up zigzagging to go up rather than knocking someone off the ladder as you go up."

Ross took a moment to say something very much worth repeating here, whether you are a highflier or someone who spots highfliers. He said, "My dad talked about you get out what you put in and achieve things from hard work. I said to my team last week, 'You all make this work. Our asset is you. I know the level of talent we have here. We have teamwork and caring. We think differently, we inspire each other. The insights we get in our conference rooms, so simple in their clarity and powerful in their process, will help us create the model for this century.'"

Now back to his description of this same highflier:

"I hire for three things: calm, curious, and a complement to the team. Those things like with culture and my highfliers tick those boxes to varying degrees. The one in my mind who I know will travel far is the curious one. I know when they go home, it is not 'I've done my job.' Some of them go home and are still reading. They are passionately curious about what they have gotten into. Do not go into something if you are going to be bored by it. If you are going into something you can be passionate about, be prepared to do all the drudgery at the bottom. Gradually the highfliers make their way up. They find that they cannot just switch off from learning about something. They enjoy thinking about it. One highflier said to me, 'You know, Ross, I think it's better for the business if James does this. And here are the reasons why including that the client has many things in common with James.' That is someone who really cares about the business and how we will succeed in that case. It is NOT 'I'm going to win this business and get a pat on the back.' It was a level of care and thoughtfulness. They knew the business would benefit if another colleague stepped in. And also it was NOT a

matter of fear or nervousness that if it did not work out there would be repercussions. That example really struck me in the moment."

Ross had so much to say about team development that he as much as gave me a short, *hip-pocket* as they say in the military, class on that as well as on highfliers. I just have to share it with you.

"We have a very, very settled team, and I think that's in our business. We have to work as a team to sort of sift through the noise of trying to find the type of company we want. You have to work together. You really must collaborate. And everyone wants their time in the spotlight. So part of my job is to put them in the spotlight now and again so they feel a bit of love. And I did that and they can look back to that as a reference point. But the risk when you have a settled team, and this is linked with critical thinking, is everyone gets on so well that you don't get challenged. You don't get this sort of, 'Oh, I'm not sure about that,' or 'You know, I really … I really disagree with that.' And several of us worked together at Newton for a decade. So our risk of groupthink, to my mind, is high. It's high. It's fundamentally and structurally high.

So, what do we do? We have a particular type of meeting. We've run this for five years. It was created to accelerate critical thinking. It was to put that in the forefront. It also allows quiet people to be able then to be seen clearly and not in the blurred background … And we, when you hire youngsters, they often don't want to talk in front of senior people, particularly if they're going to be critical. And we have a flat management structure that's meant to encourage them to be critical of what we're thinking. But we have a meeting. It's a fun name, Allen, but we have a meeting where we call it an 'espresso after the coffee.' Just a fun meeting. And what we do is we have one hour where we have one stock, so very concentrated. We attack our invest-ment thesis so nobody in the room, even the analyst who suggested it, is known to each other. We've held it for two years. The stock could have been doing great. It could have been doing poorly. We structure it where we get in a third party analyst.

So, let's say it's MasterCard. We did this once with MasterCard. We found we kept hearing about blockchain technology and how that might upset payments to current payments technology. This is about seven years ago, okay? And we said, well, fine, we heard there was a good block-chain community out in Berlin. Is it some sort of stuff you want to hear about, and by the way, we flew a guy over from Berlin who was part of a blockchain community, cryptocurrency community. They're quite messianic about what they're going to do to MasterCard, Visa, and all that stuff. And he presented to us on how blockchain cryptos will rule the world. You know, as I say, they're messianic. 'This is how the little companies are going to eventually knock MasterCard out.' We thought, well, that's interest-ing. That doesn't seem credible. We gathered our best questions and then we invited a third-party analyst into these Nespresso meetings. For one hour we're going to do nothing but attack our investment thesis on something we hold. It's just all going to be negative. The analyst isn't even allowed to defend it. I think that helps them unburden any niggling things that might have felt too stupid to defend it. And we attack and it's one of the most enjoyable meet-ings because you then get to see some of the youngsters, the future leaders. Then you get to see their line of thinking in a very comfortable environment. Someone could say, 'It could be or it might be ludicrous, but are they going to be attacked by or lose their barrier to entry because of XY?' And I find meetings like that with our young team is where we get the critical thinking. If they've not seen it before, they can learn from it and see it. And the great thing: then they must do it in the day-to-day. I think your point in critical thinking is necessary. But one of the things for me is, and this is the sign of the maturity thing, going back to the point I said at the start, it's how they do that tells me about their maturity."

The Good Ones "Just Figure It Out"

I never had to think about "saving the best for last" because all of them were nothing but the best. Let's just say the most recent one introduced two notions about highfliers that were so interesting. One was the hypothesis that starting in sales has real advantages. The other is the notion of "just figure it out."

Taylor Smith recently retired as CEO from Joerns Healthcare in Charlotte, North Carolina. It was a post he held from 2020 to 2024. Taylor successfully led the business through the impact of COVID-19 and the knock-on effects of the global supply chain disruption. He executed a material restructuring of the business, divesting lower profit segments, while relaunching the capital products business in North America. In conjunction with the Board of Directors he partnered with investment banks executing several strategic divestitures.

Taylor had this to say:

"I've got the person for you. I've hired him twice in my career. I was the sales leader at Cardinal Health. There

was a person who was in area sales. Then I was promoted to my first general manager role. I had seen them in the sales organization. I thought, 'This person has huge headroom.' And I do not think they saw it in themselves. We talked about this at one time ... about 'where do you want your career to go?' They wanted to stay in sales their whole career. I said, 'You can do more.' I had an open marketing role and convinced them to come in to this role, almost against their will. We had a good relationship. What I saw was a person who was smarter than he thought he was. He was a humble guy. I think he knew he was a good sales leader but I thought he was much more than that. I said, 'You know the customer. You know the market. You're really smart. You have a great gut about you.' They had the intuition you cannot teach. He had great followership, vertically and horizontally. They were just one of those people that everybody liked and everyone respected. I do not think, though, that they were seen as a riser. Maybe they were too nice. Maybe it's one of those perception things that we've all seen a million times.

I said to them, 'This will change you. It's a global marketing job.' They said, 'I don't think I'm qualified.' I said, 'But I know you are.' I could have chosen someone else. We interviewed others. And guess what? They crushed the interviews and won the job. They did that job for four years. They said to me recently, 'It changed the trajectory of my life.' They saw all those things in themselves that I saw. They were put into a totally different side of the business. As you well know, Allen, marketing is not sales. It is a very different discipline and that is especially true in international marketing.

It was great watching them grow and flourish. All the things I saw were on display. It was one of those gut calls as a brand-new general manager. I trusted them. It was the first pick I got a chance to make. And it was a great one."

A Few Final Thoughts About Strategic Thinking

For 40+ years, I've had the pleasure of knowing, and sometimes collaborating with, a psychologist who advises his clients on a variety of issues including hiring and promotion decisions. He is a remarkable observer and listener as he interviews people and offers insights to their boards of directors about how they think and their potential for significant positions in his clients' company. He asked for anonymity, and I agreed to it given the national and international assignments he continues to have.

I decided to focus our time together on the topic of strategic thinking. Here's what he told me.

"You know the first thing I thought about that makes me suspect that the person is strategic and high potential is that by the end of the interview, I learned something I didn't know before. It was never about the content of their job but they expanded my thinking in one way, shape, or form. It could be about a process or it could be about the industry in which they work. It could be about leadership or even about life. It could be about philosophy. But I learn something that I didn't know about before. I consider myself reasonably worldly and somewhat knowledgeable, and if this person teaches me something I didn't know, it makes me perk up that this is an interesting person who thinks in

a way I haven't thought. And that correlates in my mind with thinking broadly or, if we use that terminology, strategically. So ... that's a big one.

Conversely if at the end of the interview I saw someone who was competent with a terrific resume and gave me 'all the right answers' and was also a good communicator, it seemed routine in the sense that I didn't learn much. Then that person would be marked down in my mind in the area of strategic thinking.

I've probably done thousands of interviews over the years. This quality of 'teaching' is most certainly not in a didactic form. It's never as if they say, 'Let me tell you something about, let's say AI, that you didn't know before.' It's usually a rejoinder, a reaction to something I would say. When I've been in meetings and see a variety of people, there may be a CEO and maybe an executive vice president, maybe some junior people who I didn't know. What sparks the thought that this person may have strategic potential or might be high potential is usually a comment that is not a part of a presentation. It's usually in terms of a comment they may volunteer, maybe one where they would take some risk to say in a meeting with someone more senior. Chances are it's an off-the-cuff remark more than something that was planned but they are willing to take the risk and they have the insight to say something that wasn't brought up before and that the listeners didn't know about."

Refer back to Chapter 2 and Bob Azelby's interview. His example of a highflier showing strategic thinking falls exactly into what the industrial psychologist is talking about: not the planned presentation but a question with an answer that is somewhat risky.

The psychologist and I talked for a while about a client we both served at the same time. In thinking about the people we worked with there, he said:

"There were multiple businesses within the larger business. There was a strategy for each one of them. Many of the people we worked with then, Allen, were strategic in the sense that they were running their individual departments in concert with the larger company broad strategy. As I think about it, they were more savvy tacticians who knew the strategy and knew what would work politically inside a larger complex organization. But the exceptional ones, who end up being CEOs themselves, will reach beyond the business strategy. They are strategic because they are so far sighted.

At lower levels, however, a junior person or even a middle level manager, the things they say usually involve some risk taking. It takes some courage to say something and that, I'd say, is a difference between people who are higher potential and those who aren't. They will say something in the right way. They will say it in a way that provokes further thought and that people in the audience will say to themselves, 'Wow. I wouldn't have thought of that before if it weren't for Joe or Sally making that comment. It takes some risk.'

Related to your work, Allen, is the ability to distill things in everyday terms so that even someone who is a complete novice could understand. People who are strategic, even at a junior level, an entry level, a fresh out of college level have an ability to clearly see and speak to what the key points of a problem are. They distill it down. They see things other people don't see because of their clear vision of what's happening and they can communicate about it clearly.

I saw them so many times mentoring people who were not their direct reports. They just helped people. They would see someone in their orbit, say someone not doing particularly well and felt they could help them. They might actually say, 'If you don't mind and I can speak into your life a little bit...' Just a genuinely good person. Now they are a big deal at Microsoft. They've had a fantastic career.

I just wonder if you can teach all this. That is partly a result of how he was raised. They were always trying to be a servant leader as time went on. Not always perfect, but well, you know..."

References

Abrahams, M. and Immelt, J. (2021). Leading from the hot seat: how to communicate under pressure. Stanford Business School. The Podcast, June 25, 2021.

Abrahams, R. and Groysberg, B. (2021). How to become a better listener. *Harvard Business Review Digital Articles*. December 21, 2021.

Albarracin, D. and Shavitt, S. (2018). Attitudes and attitude change. *Annual Review of Psychology*, 69: 299–327.

Bates (2021). Executive presence: a model of highly effective leadership [online]. Available from bates company [accessed August 2024]

Burgoon, J.K., Guerrero, L.K., and Floyd, K. (2016). *Nonverbal Communication*. Routledge.

Burgoon, M. and Ruffner, M. (1977). *Human Communication*. Winston, NY: Holt, Rinehart, 72.

Covey, S.R. (1989). *The Seven Habits of Highly Effective People: Restoring the Character Ethic*. New York: Simon and Schuster.

Feintzeig, R. (2024). Is "rizz" the secret to getting ahead at work? *Wall Street Journal*, 21 July, 2024.

Frandsen, F. and Johansen, W. (2020). Crisis Communication. *The International Encyclopedia of Organizational Communication*, p. 493. DeGruyter Mouton.

Funk, K. (1997). Implications of political expertise in candidate trait evaluations. *Political Research Quarterly*, 50: 675–697.

Gallo, A. (2024). What is active listening. *Harvard Business Review Digital Articles*. October 21, 2024.

Golden, J. (1997). The issue of character in the presidential contest of 1996. *American Behavioral Scientist*, 40: 994–1000.

References

Hallahan et al. (2007). Defining Strategic Communication, *International Journal of Strategic Communication* 1 (1): 3–35.

Hanford, P. (1995). Developing director and executive competencies in strategic thinking. In: *Developing Strategic Thought: Reinventing the Art of Direction-Giving* (ed. B. Garratt), 157–186. London: McGraw-Hill.

Hewlett, S. (2024). Executive presence. Thrive Street Advisors [online]. Available from: Leadership Library [accessed August 2024].

Hovland, C.I., Janis, I.L., and Kelley, H.H. (1953). *Communication and Persuasion*. Yale University Press.

Jachimowicz, Wihler, and Galinsky (2020, November). My boss' passion matters as much as my own: the interpersonal dynamics of passion are a critical driver of performance evaluations. *Journal of Organizational Behavior* 43 (9); 1496–1515.

Joly, H. and Lambert, C. (2021). *The Heart of Business—Leadership Principles for the Next Era of Capitalism*. Boston, MA: Harvard Business Review Press.

Kinder, D. (1986). Presidential character revisited. In: *Political Cognition: The 19th Annual Carnegie Symposium on Cognition* (eds. R. Lau and D. Sears). Hillsdale, NJ: Erlbaum.

Kraus, S., Harms, R., and Schwarz, E.J. (2006). Strategic planning in small enterprise, new empirical findings. *Management Research News* 29 (6): 334–344.

Levine, T.R. and Park, H.S. (2017). The research of James C. McCroskey: a personal and professional remembrance. *Communication Research Reports*, 34 (4): 376–380.

Macht, G. and Nembhard, D. (2015). Measures and models of personality and their effects on communication and team performance. *International Journal of Industrial Ergonomics*. 49. 10.1016/j.ergon.2015.05.00

McAdam, R. and Bailie, C. (2002). Business performance measure and alignment impact on strategy. *International Journal of Operations and Production Management* 22 (1): 972–996.

McCroskey, J. and Young, T. (1981). Ethos and credibility: the construct and its measurement after three decades. *Central States Speech Journal* 32: 24.

References

McCroskey, J.C and Tevan, J.J. (1999). Goodwill: a reexamination of the construct and its measurement, *Communication Monographs* 66 (1): 90–103.

Mehrabian, A. (1972). *Nonverbal Communication*, 1e. Routledge.

Morgan, (2020). *The Future Leader*, 17–18. Hoboken, New Jersey J: Wiley.

Mui, C. (2024). Celebrating the LifeBits of Gordon Bell, LinkedIn, May 20, 2024.

Navarro, J. (2021). The primacy of emotions. *Psychology Today*, American Psychological Association, [online].

Netta, A., Gates, L., Lawrence, M. et al. (April 2021). Social Science Research Modules Project. [Online] Middlebury College.

Polboon N., Ilkka, K., and Igel, B. (2013). A new model of strategic thinking competency. *Journal of Strategy and Management* 6 (3): 242–264.

Richmond, B. (March 1997). The systems thinker. *Pegasus Communication* 8 (2).

Rogers, C.R. and Farson, R.E. (1987). *Communicating in Business Today*. Excerpt from ACTIVE LISTENING Communicating in Business Today R.G. Newman, M.A. Danzinger, M. Cohen (eds.). D.C. Heath & Company.

Schneider, W. (1996). Choosing performance over character. *National Journal*, 28: 30–31.

Stevenson, R.L. (1886). *The Strange Case of Dr. Jekyll and Mr. Hyde*. London: Longmans, Green, and Co.

McCroskey, Hamilton, and Weiner (1974). The Effect of Interaction Behavior on Source Credibility, Homophily, and Interpersonal Attraction: 42–52.

Thomas and Znaniecki (1918–1920). *The Polish Peasant in Europe and America*. Boston: R. G. Badger.

Vaghefi, R. and Heullmantel, A. (1990). *Strategic Management for the XXIst Century*, 435–461. CRC Press.

Acknowledgments

Everyone who has worked with CDA in any capacity knows there's no CDA much less this book without Marie Lopez. A few years ago when Marie was pregnant with Gianna, I got a call from a woman who had retired from one of our clients in Colorado. She called to tell me a story about Marie. I was due to arrive at the client site one morning to facilitate a seminar and this woman was hosting me. She had tried to reach me but couldn't so she called Marie's cell. Marie answered and said, "Can I call you back in 10? I'm in labor." That's Marie. They say no one is unreplaceable. Marie cannot be replaced.

I need to thank Marc Mikulich, my agent, and Malcolm Kushner, who recommended Marc to me. I get the biggest thrill out of even saying the words, "My agent said ..." Marc was enthusiastic about my idea for this book and that gave me the impetus I needed.

Thank you to all the executives who gave their time and effort in our interviews. I know how busy they are, but they were more than happy to tell me their highflier stories. I'm flattered they all took my call and responded with so much enthusiasm.

Thank you to my editor Georgette Beatty. I knew that every suggestion she made was in the spirit of making *The Highflier Handbook* a better book. And so it is.

I'm indebted to thousands of companies and the people working at those companies who invited me into their world to speak and

Acknowledgments

give advice over and over again. Their honest feedback keeps me on track and that includes suggestions that led to *The Highflier Handbook*.

The team at Wiley including Zachary Schisgal and Amanda Pyne made me feel like a part of the family from the first message I received that started with "Congratulations." It's such pure pleasure to say "Wiley" when I'm asked who my publisher is.

Thank you to the professors who took me under their wing and taught me proper, disciplined, and scholarly research at the Master's and PhD level, both at West Virginia University and at the University of Southern California, particularly Ken Sereno who has regularly invited me back to USC to talk to his classes.

My mom and dad were fortunate enough to leave Poland and start their American life in Charleston, West Virginia. I am a product of their pioneer spirit and have no doubts at all that my career as a consultant could not have started without their hugs. And that extends to all my friends from childhood in Charleston who set the bar for friendship and support. A very special shoutout to Chic Krukiel, who was my first reader and editor.

About the Author

ALLEN WEINER is the Managing Director of Communication Development Associates, Inc. in Woodland Hills, California. He was one of the founders of the firm, which was constituted in 1976, and has since served as counsel to senior management on a variety of issues related to human communication. Allen's external responsibilities include on-site delivery of seminars and individualized coaching. Internally, he serves on the long-term planning committee and leads the research and development group.

Allen completed Bachelor's and Master's degrees in Communication at West Virginia University. He served in the U.S. Navy on destroyers and cruisers during the Vietnam War era. Following his service, he received his PhD in Communication Studies from The Annenberg School of Communication at the University of Southern California. His research interests were and remain persuasion and influence, interpersonal attraction, and credibility, and he has several published studies on those topics.

Communication Development Associates' clients have included the Jet Propulsion Lab, Lawrence Berkeley National Laboratory, geophysicists at the world's leading energy companies, research and development leaders in pharmaceuticals, IT professionals in a wide variety of settings, and legal scholars and practicing attorneys at several worldwide law firms.

About the Author

Allen's book *So Smart But...: How Intelligent People Lose Credibility—and How They Can Get it Back* (Jossey-Bass, 2006) has been described as "required reading for all leaders who want to protect and extend the most valuable personal asset they have."

Allen is married to Carol Weiner. Their son, Matt, is Co-founder and CEO of MegaFire Action.

In 2011, Allen received the Eberly College of Arts and Sciences Distinguished Alumni award given by West Virginia University where he received his BA and MA.

Index

Index

Index

Index